MW00340046

SMOKED FOOD

SMOKED FOOD

James Strawbridge

A MANUAL FOR HOME SMOKING

First published in 2019

A catalogue record for this book is available
from the British Library.

ISBN 978 1 78521 217 8

Library of Congress control number
2018938910

Photography: Simon Burt
Additional photographs: p34 Stephen Pennells,
p35, 38 (bl) 41 Kamodo Joe, p36 (tl) ProQ,
p36 (tr) Bradley Smoker.
Art direction and food styling: James Strawbridge
Book design: Adelle Mahoney

Published by Haynes Publishing,
Sparkford, Yeovil, Somerset BA22 7JJ, UK.
Tel: 01963 440635
Int. tel: +44 1963 440635
Website: www.haynes.com

Haynes North America Inc.,
859 Lawrence Drive, Newbury Park,
California 91320, USA.

Printed in Malaysia.

CONTENTS

INTRODUCTION

I've been smoking food in earnest for the last 20 years, but I feel that I still have more to learn and recipes to experiment with. When I first started, I researched traditional methods in old books and visited smokehouses around the UK, observing various methods and trying out what I'd seen at home. Watching others is a great starting point for developing a new skill, and the interesting thing about smoking food is that much of the inherited knowledge and old techniques have faded from cook books. Instead, they are kept alive by artisan experts and home-smoking enthusiasts. Things are changing, though, and both professional chefs and keen home cooks are working to fill this gap in their knowledge and reignite a primal passion for all things smoked. I hope that this book provides interesting ideas and an introduction to smoking methods for both groups.

My initial introduction to smoking food came was when I was eight or nine years old and I helped build a smoker with my dad. We cut up an old oil drum, cleaned it out and started cold smoking cheese and eggs most weekends. The taste of home-smoked Cheddar with sliced apple on crackers is one of my enduring food memories and I can still clearly conjure up the dense smoke flavour that permeated deep into the cheese. Since then my culinary journey has taken me on a long and winding road, from working the fields to professional kitchens. In my 20s I started growing and rearing most of my own food on a self-sufficient farm in Cornwall and with that came a range of skills, from making cheese to baking, preserving the harvest, to butchery. These skills equipped me with an insight into how to work with ingredients and bring out the best in them. As a professional chef, smoking and curing have always held a special place in my knife roll. The skills are so wonderfully instinctive and sensory. The smell, appearance, texture and taste all transform food with serious wow factor. If you choose to learn one new cookery skill I seriously suggest that smoking food should be a contender. You can neither replicate the same degree of theatrical results, nor make the same pronounced changes in flavour of a raw ingredient, unless you cure and smoke it.

I wrote my first book on this subject several years ago and ever since then I've been busy putting my smoked food on to restaurant menus and into supermarkets, and have been running workshops on the subject. The thing that has struck me most on my journey is that everyone has a smoked food story or a fresh perspective. Try out new flavour combinations that you hear about for yourself at home. Share your recipes with friends and visit food festivals for inspiration. Use this book as a starting point to grasp the basics, gain confidence and then adapt the dishes to suit your taste.

Remember, though, that smoked food is a specialist subject and the key principles and basic science that I cover are based on years of personal experience, so it's best not to ignore them. I don't want to be too prescriptive, but equally I hope this manual will provide all the guidance you need to safely learn the art of different kinds of curing, drying, smoking and grilling over flames. Many of the dishes are classic crowd-pleasers that every smoked-food fan will want to master – things like brisket, burnt ends or chicken wings – but there are others that are more unusual and innovative. So have fun, and remember that if you're not smiling then you're doing it wrong!

JAMES STRAWBRIDGE

HISTORY OF SMOKING

The tradition of smoking food spans thousands of years and is part of our cooking heritage around the world, from transforming the humble jalapeño into a Mexican chipotle to smoking hops for a specialist German beer, and making local delicacies such as smoked llama in the Andes or British kippers for breakfast. For me, the history of smoking and curing food provides a valuable insight into our past relationship with food and fire, as well as offering up inspiration that enables us to fuse a modern perspective with ancient techniques. The future of smoked food is looking exciting as top chefs and home cooks rediscover the almost magical power of smoke.

ANCIENT HISTORY

As a history graduate, one of the things I loved about studying was that you are afforded more time to imagine the past and piece together fragments of artefacts or carbon-dated clues to form your own picture. The general consensus, based on archeological evidence, is that smoking food is the oldest form of flavouring meat and fish, and dates back to the time when early man harnessed fire for warmth and for cooking. One theory is that meat or fish that was being dried to preserve it was placed near smoke in order to keep away flies, or perhaps the method arose from mere happy accident – the result of someone leaving some flesh near a fire and waking up the next morning to a smoky breakfast treat.

Either way, the reality is that the combination of wood combustion with meat and smoke creates a layer of magic that not only tastes great, but also keeps meat edible for much longer. In a time when hunter-gatherers had no other viable means of storing food, this would have been a lifesaver, and I therefore think we can confidently surmise that Neolithic communities would have quickly realised the benefits of smoking, and made it an important part of the process of sharing and preserving the spoils of a hunting or fishing trip for a nomadic lifestyle.

Fast-forward several millennia to around 3500BC and the technique was still very much in use; we know that Sumerians smoked fish, and in ancient Rome smoked cheese was often stored in cool caves and cellars, while salt pork was exported from Gaul to Rome. In China, meanwhile, under the Tang Dynasty, smoked apricots were a favourite royal treat, and lapsang souchong remains a popular smoked tea today.

Personally, I'm genuinely fascinated by the fact that people have been smoking meats and fish for so long, using methods that haven't changed too much. The connection with smoke and fire is still as mesmerising now as it would have been then, and it is a privilege to be able to engage with this most instinctive form of cooking, not out of necessity, as they would have, but for pure enjoyment.

MODERN HISTORY

Preserving food by salting or drying, or both, continued to be one of the common ways to preserve food right up until the early 20th century. If the food was meat or fish, it was often also smoked in addition to being dried and salted; indeed, before the 17th century, almost every farmstead in North America and Europe had a smokehouse. Then, in the 19th century, the technology of canning foods,

Swede ate gravlax, considerable risk would have been involved. However, weighed against the certain dangers of starvation, it was deemed worth it.

Today, fermentation is no longer used in the process of making gravlax. Instead, the salmon is 'buried' in a dry marinade of salt, sugar and dill, and cured for a few days. As the fish cures, by the action of osmosis, the moisture turns the dry cure into a concentrated brine that can be used in Scandinavian cooking as part of a sauce.

Arbroath smokies

There are several theories about the true origin of the Arbroath smokie. One of the most popular of these relates to a cottage in which haddocks were hanging up to be dried for preservation purposes. Unfortunately, a fire broke out and burned the house to the ground. It was reputedly then, while sifting through the ashes, wood, dust and associated debris, that the 'smokies' were discovered. However, it stretches the imagination somewhat to believe that having just seen their house destroyed, the occupants (or anyone else) would pick up a dust-covered incinerated fish and eat it!

Whatever its origin, what we do know is that the process of making the smokies involved fishwives smoking the fish on sticks placed on halved whisky barrels with fires underneath, so that the smoke was trapped under layers of coarse sacking, provided by the jute mills in the local area – a technique that is very similar to one typical of communities in Scandinavia. Who knows, maybe that fabled villager had some connection with the lands of ice and snow?

Smoked salmon

Smoked salmon was first brought to the UK – to London's East End – by East European immigrants in the late 1800s. In the early days, the East London smokers imported salmon for smoking

originally developed in France in 1795, began to spread throughout much of the world, offering an alternative means of preservation. Furthermore, the old-fashioned icebox came into general use at about the same time and meant that householders could store fresh foods in their natural state for that little bit longer. Later, from the 1930s onwards, the electric refrigerator and home freezer appeared, and at the same time constantly improving transportation systems throughout the world allowed the rapid distribution of fresh meats.

All of these developments caused a decline in the number of people who did their own smoking. This was exacerbated by the growth of commercial meat processors, who began to produce the most popular smoked or cured items, such as salami, cheese, ham, bacon and sausages, using liquid smoke flavouring instead of true smoking.

As the mass production of these 'smoked' foods proliferated, the salting, smoking and drying of meat, poultry and fish by individuals began to be more of a hobby than a necessary chore. Nevertheless, many people remained in love with the flavour of properly smoked foods, and kept the tradition alive after World War II. What's more, as people in the latter half of the 20th century had increased leisure time on their hands, many began to

barbecue foods outdoors. Having discovered that they liked these grilled foods, some then wanted an even smokier result. This led them to put a cover over their traditional kettle barbecue so it functioned as a hot smoker, and smoker cookers – usually operated on charcoal and with tight-fitting lids – duly became more widespread in the 1970s with the rise of home-brewing and a resurgence of artisan crafts. With this innovation, the smoking of foods became a recognised hobby that is still enjoyed by many today.

CURED AND SMOKED FISH
Gravlax

The Scandinavian word gravlax literally means 'buried salmon' – a name that exactly describes how it was traditionally made. To store the abundant produce of summer for a long time without using much salt or other (at that time) expensive preservatives, the fish was wrapped in birch bark and buried in the ground, where a wet, cold environment and a lack of oxygen made it ferment but not rot. Nowadays, we don't regard fish that has been buried in the ground as safe to eat, although the slightly acidic birch bark does bring down the pH and thus presents a certain barrier against spoilage. Nevertheless, each time a 15th-century Norwegian or

from the Baltic, not realising that wild salmon was available from Scotland, although they later did source it from there. Part of the art of its production was the ability to smoke the salmon enough to preserve it, but not so much that it created an overpowering flavour. This stood in contrast to the Scottish tradition, which at the time was for more heavily smoked fish, such as kippers or Arbroath smokies. The Scots did not generally smoke salmon.

Pilchards

Where I live in Cornwall, we have a rich history of curing and preserving fish with salt. In fact, since 1555, when exports were first recorded, Cornish pilchards have been salted whole in bulk, then pressed and packed into wooden barrels and boxes and sold throughout Europe. This industry continued for several hundred years and at the beginning of the 20th century, there were dozens of plants salting pilchards in Cornwall, supplying the booming Italian, French and Spanish markets where they were sold from travelling carts in the remote rural regions. In Italy, which remains the primary market for salted pilchards

today, they were used in rustic dishes as the most economical salted fish to give flavour to the staple diet of pasta or polenta.

By the 1960s, however, with the rise in popularity and availability of fresh and frozen fish, only one plant continued to pack salt pilchards in Cornwall, and the industry went into decline. Today, fortunately, things are starting to go full circle and cured fish companies are gaining ground. I find it really encouraging that some Michelin-starred chefs and restaurants are putting cured fish, even the humble sardine or mackerel, on their menus again, celebrating our curing past.

CURED AND SMOKED MEAT

Native American Indian traditions

Before refrigeration it would have been essential for hunters to preserve their kill and make the most out of every part – this was a time of genuine nose-to-tail eating. Typically, when smoking meat, the Native American Indians would cut it into strips and place it on a rack, where it would be first hung and later smoked. This not only gave the meat a fantastic flavour, but it was also a great way of preserving it for quite some

time. What's more, unlike drying, which causes many meats to develop a dry, somewhat tough texture, the smoke enabled it to remain pliant.

The fires that were used to smoke the meat were not generally large. Instead, wood was commonly laid upon embers in order to keep a fire going and produce light fumes. It has also been recorded that some Plains Indian communities smoked their meat at the top of their tipis so that the wood smoke from the central fire could slowly dry it and impart flavour.

JERKY AND BILTONG

The origins of biltong – a Dutch mash-up word of *bil* meaning 'rump' and *tong* meaning 'tongue' or 'strip' – can be traced to the native Khoikhoi people of south-western Africa, who preserved meat from the large game population in the region by slicing it into strips, curing it with salt and hanging it up to dry. When Dutch settlers arrived in the mid-17th century, they needed preserved meat while they tried to build up livestock herds – a process that took years. Biltong was made by hanging meat outside for a period of about two weeks, usually during the cold winter months, which helped inhibit spoiling. The Dutch amended and appropriated the original native technique and marinated the biltong in a vinegar solution for a few hours before pouring off the liquid and seasoning the meat with a mixture of rock salt and spices, such as roasted coriander seeds, black pepper, cloves and brown sugar. In addition to providing great flavour, vinegar is a great inhibitor of bacteria while the spices, especially coriander seeds, all have antimicrobial properties. The latter were available to the Dutch because of their trade with Asian communities.

History then points to the Voortrekkers, a group of Dutch pioneers on the move, spreading the popularity of biltong to the north in the 1800s, and it took off from there. Today, biltong is usually made with beef and is a common snack in South Africa, as well as being sold in many other countries, too.

The North American dried meat known as jerky is very similar to South African biltong, although the latter is never smoked, while jerky sometimes is. However, it's important to realise that smoked and cured meats have emerged from all corners of the world and have a rich and diverse history. For example, in South America, *ch'arki* was made from all kinds of pounded, deboned meat, but was probably most commonly made from alpaca and llama. Meaning 'dried, salted meat' in Quechuan, *ch'arki* was shared with the Spanish conquistadors in the area, who were so impressed that they eventually brought it back to Western Europe. It is commonly believed that the word jerky is derived from the Quechua term.

Elsewhere, the smoked meats scene nowadays is full of exciting new recipes and at farmers markets and food festivals around the UK you can find award-winning charcuterie artisans selling a huge range of air-dried and smoked meats, such as rabbit, mutton,

venison, kangaroo or even locusts.

Southern states barbecue

The history of the barbecue is filled with grit and gumption. The term itself most likely came from the translated Caribbean Indian word barbacoa – a traditional Caribbean cooking form that involves wrapping meat (beef, but also goat or sheep) in leaves and then burying it in the ground over hot coals. Having been steamed in this underground oven, the meat is generally shredded and is distinctive both for its texture and of course that wonderful smoky flavour. Over time, the technique migrated to Mexico and then to the south-western USA and evolved into the more familiar method of cooking foods over an open fire. A taste for smoked meat in the USA dates back even further, though, to pioneers exploring the West who would have been heavily reliant on salted beef, jerky and other dried flesh to survive. Perhaps it is little wonder, then, that in the USA in particular the popularity of smoked food has exploded in recent years, with more and more regional specialities emerging and a strong culture of

ardent pitmasters and barbecue experts being very much present. You will find pulled pork everywhere in North Carolina, smoky brisket and short ribs cooked low and slow in Texas, sticky ribs with smoked barbecue sauce in Missouri, or pork shoulder with a dry rub and bourbon mop over in Tennessee – all made from their own distinctive recipes and established smoking methods. Then there is a growing fusion scene, with smoking recipes influenced by the Korean barbecue or Hawaiian kalua.

LOOKING TO THE FUTURE

I believe that smoked food in the future will continue to evolve and grow in popularity. As people become less connected to nature and more plugged into technology and digital devices, so the lure of the wild and good old-fashioned wood-fired cooking will grow in appeal to counter this trend. Smoking offers kids a digital detox – an opportunity to log-off, slow down and simplify.

There are some new areas of innovation that I find particularly exciting. Mixologists, for instance, are smoking water and freezing it down again to create smoked ice for use in their cocktails; world-renowned chefs are experimenting with smoked fruit and vegetables; and we are learning more about smoking with soft woods and the science involved in gaining that smoky flavour without any acrid resin by heating at the correct temperatures. An area where I believe we will see lots of new ideas is smoked desserts and taking savoury ingredients, smoking them and incorporating them into sweet puddings. The rise of technology and gastronomy will also have profoundly interesting results, although for me the future revolves around cooks rediscovering smoked food and working with fire to regain an instinctive approach to cooking food.

THE SCIENCE OF SMOKE

The days of cremated sausages burned on the grill, singed eyebrows and blindly trying to turn kebabs through a cloud of smoke are not really how we aim to cook any more. Smoking food and dealing with live fire is a genuine skill that, while it can still be instinctive, is as precise as any classical kitchen tradition. I have learned a lot about the science of smoke by reading work by food scientists such as Harold McGee, studying the Noma lab's experiments, and with good ol' trial and error. All of the techniques in this manual achieve a balance that will enhance the taste of your food instead of masking it, revealing a whole new palette of flavours.

WHAT IS SMOKE?

Simply put, smoke is created by the process of combustion. Technically, during combustion very large molecules break down from the wood into lots of very small ones. Smoke is not a simple gas, it's a mixture of three states of matter: solid, liquid and gaseous particles. In the same way that moisture condenses on a cold glass, so the tiny volatile molecules from the smoke vapour fly up into the air and condense on the surface of your food. In more scientific terms, when wood burns it produces nitrogen dioxide, which hits the food and dissolves, losing its oxygen molecules. It then becomes acidic, and tries to find something new to connect with to create more stability. What it finds in the meat is myoglobin, an oxygen- and iron-binding protein that attracts the acid and pulls it into the meat. This process is what makes your food take on those delicious smoky flavours.

HOW SMOKE PRESERVES FOOD

In the combustion cocktail of smoke from wood there are hundreds of volatile molecules, including phenols, which are disinfectants much like those used to kill germs. Eugenol is also present – a compound that has strong antibacterial qualities. These molecules settle on the surface of food, where moulds and bacteria are deposited, and serve as a shield against decay.

HOW SMOKE FLAVOURS FOODS

When you cook meat, the iron molecules oxidise and turn from red to brown in what is known as the Maillard reaction. When you smoke meat, however, instead of an abundance of oxygen molecules to turn the meat brown, there is carbon dioxide (CO_2) and nitric oxide (NO), the latter of which bond to the outside of the meat, leaving a beautiful pink ring (because the molecules just happen to be pink). The aroma molecules and gases given off through combustion don't diffuse into the meat very far – although if you're barbecuing for hours, some permeation will occur – which means that most of the flavour and colour occurs in the outer part of the food. This is known among barbecue

enthusiasts as the 'bark' or 'smoke ring' and if you manage to achieve a good thick layer, this is perceived as the mark of real smoky flavour and the result of well-spent time and effort.

FAT SCIENCE

When wood is burned it breaks down a chemical called cellulose that exists in the wood. This is then turned into sugar, which caramelises on the fat of meat or fish being cooked over the flames and helps to break it down.

Some meats, such as ribs, brisket and pork shoulder, are also full of connective tissue, which is packed with collagen. This substance, when cooked fast and on a high heat, contracts and creates a tough texture in the meat. However, if you cook collagen-rich meats low and slow, the collagen breaks down and melts. While melting, water gets into this collagen, and creates gelatine, which makes the meat tender, juicy and flavourful. This process is called rendering and it is integral to creating succulent meat.

COLD SMOKING

Cold smoking is the process of applying smoke in a chamber between 15°C and 30°C (59–86°F), so the smoked food does not cook. There are many different cold-smoking techniques, though it is widely recognised that the healthiest and most balanced in terms of flavour use indirect smoke generation. This means that the smoke is produced in an external chamber and then travels through a pipe to the chamber where the food awaits. The smoke cools down slightly during transit, with only the most volatile and delicate molecules of the burning material penetrating the food in the chamber.

The refined taste of cold smoking also depends on the humidity of the burning fuel. Wood that is too wet produces too many acids, which impart an acrid flavour. For cold smoking, the wood moisture is best when it is between 16 and 20 per cent.

The quality of the final product does not only depend on the smoke produced; the humidity of the food itself is crucial. If it is too dry, the Maillard-type reactions will not occur and the smoke will not penetrate the food. If it is too wet, it will not colour nicely due to a reduced Maillard reaction, and flavours will be absorbed unevenly. In light of this, professionals agree that the humidity in the smoking chamber should be 75–85 per cent.

*Below: **A cold smoke generator helps to achieve a perfect slow smoke.***

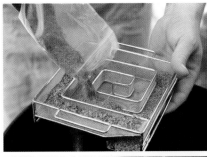

HOT SMOKING

Nowadays, smoking is not seen just as a method of preservation. More and more, it is valued for its ability to produce flavour. While cold smoking both preserves food and transmits taste, hot smoking is mainly used for flavour. With hot smoking, food is exposed to smoke for anything from a couple of minutes to a couple of hours, and the product does not dry out as much as it can through cold smoking.

For hot smoking, it is best to use wet or freshly cut wood. The latter contains 40–60 per cent moisture, so when fresh wood is not in season, you can rehydrate drier wood to this moisture content. Wet wood seems to produce more smoke, but this is not the case. The extra volume of smoke is nothing more than water vapor (steam) mixed with the same amount of smoke that is produced by drier wood. In fact, that's the main reason for using this kind of wood, as you don't want the surface of your product to dry out and harden. When the surface of the meat is softer, smoke is able to penetrate the meat more deeply. Steam from the burning wood also heats up the smoking chamber to a cooking temperature of 45–80°C/113–176°F.

BRINING

Soaking meat, fish or vegetables in a strong salt solution is one of the best ways to draw out moisture via osmosis and preserve food. It also helps to create a product that is then more open to taking on flavour from smoking. What's more, you can add powerful aromatics to the saline solution by mixing in a selection of herbs and spices, and the long soak means they really penetrate the meat or fish. Brining also hydrates the flesh, keeping it moist and juicy.

TYPES OF SALT

Salt is discussed in more detail on pages 18–19, but in brief, here are the four main types used for brining:
KOSHER – cleaner flavour, easier to dissolve, but expensive.
TABLE – easy to come by and cheap, table salt is also easy to dissolve.
ROCK SALT – harder to dissolve than table salt but can be good value.
SEA SALT – I tend not to use this for brining as it's more expensive than other types and I think the flavour can be lost slightly.

SWEET BRINES

Generally, brining is achieved with a large proportion of salt and a little sugar. However, you will find that some recipes require you to use a sweet brine cure. This is because sugar not only helps balance the salty flavours but also increases the growth of Lactobacillus – a bacteria that is beneficial to the curing process.

HOW TO MAKE A BASIC BRINE SOLUTION

Dissolve 300g/11oz/1½ cups salt in 450ml/¾ pint/scant 2 cups water. This equates to roughly 6 per cent salt to liquid and the percentage is equal to 23° on the brinometer scale (see below). Generally, you need half the volume of brine compared to the weight of the product. For red meat,

TOP TIPS
- If you are dissolving the salt in hot water, allow it to cool completely before you add the food that you are brining.
- Don't reuse brine solutions.
- Keep brining foods refrigerated, or at least below 5°C/41°F.
- Always use at least the advised percentage of salt in the saline solution.
- Change the solution regularly if you are curing a large cut of meat.

PERCENTAGES FOR SALT SOLUTIONS

Product	% salt	Brining time
Beef	20%	1 day per 1kg/2¼lb
Pork	20%	3 days per 1kg/2¼lb
Poultry	10%	Whole 12–48 hours Breast 1–2 hours
Fish	5%	1–2 hours

1 *Trim the excess fat off your joint before brining, and remove any sinew.*

2 *Make sure the brine has cooled fully before submerging the meat.*

3 *Cover the meat with a heavy plate to completely submerge it in the brine.*

4 *The meat will become significantly lighter as a result of brining.*

5 *When the brining time is over, remove the joint from the liquid and pat dry with plenty of kitchen paper. Cover with an aromatic spice rub before slow cooking.*

increase the strength significantly to 20 per cent salt to liquid, and it is also worth adding 10 per cent sugar. Allow 1 day of brining per 1kg/2¹/₄lb of meat. For poultry, use a 10 per cent salt solution, and for fish 5 per cent.

Brinometer

A technical way to measure your brine solution is to use a salinometer or brinometer. This consists of a float with a stem attached, marked in degrees. The instrument will float at its highest level in a saturated brine of 26.4 per cent salt solution, also known as a fully saturated brine. In weaker brines the stem floats at lower levels and the

reading will be lower. A salinometer's scale measures the density of a salt water solution, if you add other ingredients then the density may change but the saline ratios may not.

SPICES AND HERBS

Apart from the basics of salt, water and sometimes sugar, there are various other things you can add to your brine to inject some more flavour:
• Bay leaves • Cloves • Juniper berries
• Fresh root ginger • Coriander seeds
• Black pepper • Rosemary • Thyme
• Garlic • Star anise • Cinnamon sticks
• Lemon or orange zest • Cloves
• Fennel • Lemon grass.

BRINING TUBS

The most basic way of brining something fairly small is to use a plastic freezer container with a lid, but you can also use zip-lock bag. Make sure the bag is large enough to hold enough brining solution to surround the meat, and lay it on a tray. For bigger fish and joints, the container will obviously also need to be bigger – for a leg of ham you may want a large tub such as an ice box or a plastic basin, or even a plastic bin. The key is always to keep your food submerged and properly refrigerated – at least below 5°C/41°F is advised – and the plastic should be food safe and scrupulously cleaned.

DRY CURING

Salt is the ingredient that makes everything in this manual possible, allowing for the safe processing and consumption of all manner of foods. However, not all salt is the same, and it's worth examining the properties of the different types so you can make an informed choice about what you use.

TYPES OF SALT

Sea salt

This is the remains of evaporated seawater that is often heated in shallow salt pans until it reaches a point at which the crystals can be harvested. Sea salt contains a complex combination of magnesium, sodium chloride, calcium, iodine and potassium, the levels of which vary from place to place. I use a lot of sea salt for my curing because I love the mineral make-up, which translates to a great taste. My favourite is Cornish sea salt, which is available in fine flakes, crystals or larger sea salt flakes.

Rock salt

Rock salt is crystallised salt, also known as halite. It is often drilled out then crushed and graded several times before being bagged and sorted. It can also be produced by jetting water under high pressure into underground wells and then pumping the water to the surface as brine that is subsequently evaporated at a salt refinery. It is extremely processed, so I don't tend to use it for my curing recipes.

Himalayan salt

This naturally pink salt is high-quality and a very tasty product to cure with. I use it as a solid salt block for curing very thin slices of scallop or for salt baking steaks to season them in the oven. As a cure, I would recommend trying it as a blend with cardamom seeds for special recipes, such as those made with white fish, so the flavour can shine through.

PDV salt

Pure dried vacuum (PDV) salt is salt that has been made by evaporating brine in a vacuum, which produces granules that are very fine and as pure as 99.9 per cent. This kind of salt is perfect for large salt-box curing and ensuring an even distribution during commercial curing.

Fleur de sel

This premium French product is regarded as a high-quality sea salt and often has a grey tinge of colour to it. It tastes great but the texture can be quite hard and similar to rock crystals rather than flakes. It is also very expensive, so it's best reserved for seasoning rather than curing

Kosher salt

Kosher salt itself is not actually a kosher product; instead, it is a high-grade, large-sized salt crystal that draws

DAILY DRY CURING

1 *Use both sugar and salt for the cure mix for a sweet, balanced flavour.*

2 *Grind whole spices before mixing to release their flavour.*

3 *Use a piece of meat that has been air dried, and pat it dry before curing.*

4 *Use glass or ceramic rather than metal containers to avoid corrosion.*

5 *Keep the cure in an airtight container to keep the flavours fresh.*

6 *Massage into the meat, and cure in a ziplock bag for easy draining.*

moisture and blood away from meat to bring it in line with the required preparation of kosher meat.

Celery salt
This salt can be a natural alternative for some commercial cures since celery contains lots of nitrates as well as antioxidants, which help your body process the nitrates. The downside of using celery salt in cures is that it's hard to guess how much nitrate it contains as there is no regulation in place. I often use some in my salamis, along with other salt.

Pink salt or Prague powder
Pink salt is very different from naturally occurring Himalayan salt as it contains nitrites and nitrates. The colour is added to clearly differentiate it from normal table salt.

CURE #1 This is a mixture of sodium nitrite and sodium chloride that is used for curing whole muscles that are then cold smoked – meat such as bacon and ham. The nitrite can get used up relatively quickly in curing so it is not advisable to use it for foods with long curing times.

CURE #2 Sodium nitrate, sodium

nitrite and sodium chloride mixed together provide a fast-acting cure to protect against botulism. It is often used in salami that is cured over a longer time period and never on products that will be heated to a high temperature, such as bacon, because it can then form nitrosamines, which have carcinogenic properties.

NITRATES AND NITRITES
The commercial meat-curing industry uses nitrates and nitrites in their processing to avoid botulism and prevent the growth of harmful

bacteria; it is the only guaranteed way to be absolutely sure that botulism can't take hold, so they use it out of necessity. These nitrates and nitrites also fix a deep colour in sausages and other commercially produced meats that you won't get by curing them more naturally, hence the difference in appearance between something bought in a store and made at home.

Personally, I do not use nitrates and nitrites for my curing recipes because I believe that by adhering to reliable traditional knowledge, using the correct quantity of salt, hanging products in ideal air-drying conditions, adopting good hygiene practices and only using top-quality ingredients you don't need artificial preservatives for home curing. The key to food safety is to pay close attention to factors of temperature, humidity and acidity at all times. If in doubt, never risk it.

The other main reason that I avoid using nitrates and nitrites in my curing is because there are major concerns over the carcinogenic properties of the nitrosamines that can be released when foods containing these substances are exposed to high heat.

Research is ongoing, but since I don't need to use nitrites or nitrates I feel it's best to simply avoid them altogether.

DRY CURING

Packing meat or fish in salt is the oldest and simplest way to preserve meat and fish, and over time we've learned to include sugar, herbs, spices and other ingredients to add flavour and, in the case of sugar, counteract the loss of colour that can occur.

On a basic level, when salt is rubbed into meat or fish it draws out the water – this process is called osmosis – and inhibits the growth of enzymes and microbes. Enzymes can trigger the rotting process, so the simplest way to stop them is to freeze, cook or cure food. The curing process must also effectively stop unwashed bacteria from forming.

The pH level also plays an important role, but it is easier to rely on a safe salt percentage to keep cured foods fit for consumption. It is important to remember that meat is vulnerable to the start of decomposition during the curing process, so it must always be kept in a cool place.

Although this may sound scary, the process of dry curing is actually the most accessible starting point for preserving your own food and is a key skill to master before you start smoking it. What's more, the reward for what is in reality relatively little work is a truly wonderful end product. There is nothing quite like a rasher (strip) of home-cured bacon sizzling in the pan to bring a smile to your face and give you confidence, especially when you compare it to a brine-injected rasher from the supermarket that leaches out grey water and doesn't ever seem to change colour. The two are at opposite ends of the culinary spectrum.

Daily dry curing

To dry cure you will need an appropriate food-standard tray or plastic box and it is best to store this in the fridge or in conditions below 5°C/41°F. You can also use plastic zip-lock bags or ceramic pots. First, cover your food with cure and rub it into the surface of the meat or fish, then replace the cure several times during the curing process. It is really important to ensure that your cure comprises at

SALT BOX METHOD

1 *Skewer the meat to allow the cure and flavour to penetrate the skin.*

2 *Use plenty of aromatic herbs and grated citrus zest for extra flavour, and cover the meat completely.*

3 *After curing is finished, wash the meat under cold running water to avoid it tasting too salty.*

least 2 per cent weight of salt to the weight of the meat or fish (up to 5 per cent salt is my maximum level to keep the food palatable).

Personally, I like this approach best – making up my special batch of cure, which can then be used for other products, and applying it to the surface of the food on a daily basis. Each day you will notice the liquid pulled from the meat or fish will pool in the tray and need to be poured away. Less and less will come out each time and the texture of the flesh will get firmer and the colour will become darker. It's a science lesson, too – you are observing the process of osmosis in action.

DRY CURING FISH

The simplest cure for fish, and the one I use most often, is a 50:50 mix of granulated brown sugar and coarse sea salt or rock salt (avoid fine salt – it creates an aggressive cure that leaves the fish too salty). Feel free to experiment by adding more flavours; coarse ground black pepper, citrus zest, herbs and spices all work well. Just stick to one or two, though, so the flavours don't get muddled.

Once you have mixed the cure, sprinkle a layer into a plastic or ceramic container, place the fish on top and sprinkle over some more of the cure. Generally, a handful of cure will be enough for a couple of small fish, a mackerel or a salmon fillet steak. Cover and place in the fridge overnight. Remove from the fridge, rinse off the cure, and pat dry with kitchen paper. Place back in the fridge, uncovered, for a minimum of 6–8 hours to allow the pellicle to form - this is a sticky, salty surface layer that helps the smoke particles stick to the fish.

Salt-box method

Another excellent method for curing is to put some cure in the bottom of a plastic box, place the meat or fish on top, then spread the cure all over the product, turning it to get a good even coating across the surface. This is especially good for foods that are then finished off by air drying or smoking.

Below: The magical process of turning pork into cured ham in Parma, Italy.

Total immersion method

This is an expensive and long curing process that is most popular for Parma-style ham, before it is air dried. It requires lots of salt: in the region of 20kg/44lb for a small leg of pork. Other than this, though, the technique itself is relatively straightforward. Start by finding a large plastic food container and pour in one-third of the salt. Use a plastic box so that you can see through to make sure there are no gaps where

the joint is exposed. Next, place the meat on top and completely cover it with the rest of the salt, and apply a little pressure on top with another bag of salt. For this method there is no need to empty off liquid as it will get absorbed into the salt. When the ham has lost 30 per cent of its original weight it will be ready to eat. As a rule of thumb, cure for at least 3 days for every 1kg/2¼lb of pork and then air dry for 6–12 months.

AIR DRYING

Air drying is pretty much as simple as it sounds. The basic technique is to hang food outside so that the air can pass over it and draw out any moisture, thus preventing the growth of unwanted bacteria and fungi. The key to effective drying is good air circulation, a fairly constant temperature and avoiding direct contact with moisture.

HOW TO AIR DRY FOOD

Drying is one of the cheapest and most simple ways to preserve produce. In hot countries, foods can often be effectively sun-dried (think tomatoes, chillies, fish), but in the UK and other cooler, damper countries we rely heavily on good ventilation and a slower process.

Before hanging food outside and preparing to air dry it, it is important to give it a head start by curing it to draw out some moisture. This is especially true in temperate regions. The curing process can be achieved by brining or dry curing, as already discussed, and the time that needs to be allowed for the osmosis to occur varies depending on the product. Smaller cuts of bacon, for instance, obviously need less time to cure than a large leg of ham, although both need the correct amount of salt to aid the process. Once the salt cure has done its work, however, it is time to scrub off any salt or wash off the brine solution. You then need to make sure that the joint is patted dry thoroughly before you can move on to wrapping.

What you choose to wrap your chosen item in is almost as important as where you put it. I use muslin sheets because they are cheap, easy to find at a fabric store and allow a really good flow of air. Another material that works very well is fine cloth netting, which is available online and from specialist kitchen stores. Use string to secure the parcel, and try not to overwrap it, in terms both of how much fabric you use and how tightly you wrap it, or the air won't be able to circulate.

Then all you need to do is find the perfect spot, hang the food and leave it to dry out. The longer you leave it, the longer it will keep and the more intense the flavour of the end product. It is important to check on your food regularly, for signs of rotting as well as nibbling by an unwelcome diner, and do remember to trust your nose: if it smells off, don't eat it.

HANGING TIMES

Food type	Hanging time
Air-dried ham	4–18 months
Mojama	1 month
Bresaola	3 weeks
Jerky	2 weeks
Mutton	1 month
Salami	1–2 months
Bacon/pancetta	1 week

1 *Only air dry meat that is in good condition and has been cured first.*

2 *Use muslin to wrap the meat in two layers, allowing airflow.*

3 *Use butchers twine to tie the muslin in place, but not too tightly.*

WHERE TO HANG FOODS

Finding the ideal place in which to hang foods requires a bit of care, as there are several criteria that need to be met:

· Hang in a cool place under cover, not in full sunshine but also not in complete darkness.
· If possible, use an area where a fairly constant temperature – average 10–18˚C/50–65˚F – can be maintained.
· Don't go for a corner; choose somewhere with good all-round air circulation – ideally with a through draught.
· Humidity should be between 60 and 80 per cent.
· Make sure that there are always gaps between hanging produce – i.e not touching each other.
· Hang food high enough to be out of reach of cats, dogs and children.

Drying box

Make yourself a drying box if you don't have an undercover barn or lean-to. A simple design that we like has a fly mesh or fine material on the sides, a wooden roof to deflect rain and a strong hook that enables us to hang the box from the eaves of a house or from a tree branch. Try to make the box large enough so that no part of the produce is in direct contact with it – it should be suspended inside. Alternatively, you could try to adapt an old cheese safe and then hang that up. Whatever you use, the bottom line is: make sure that air can circulate but insects and squirrels can't get in!

Dehydrators

A more expensive way to dry out foods is to buy a dehydrator – a specialist piece of equipment that creates the perfect environment for drying, with internal ventilation and variable temperature control. If you want to build your own, you could take an old cupboard or fridge, install some wire shelving and then plug in an electric fan at the bottom. Cut a few holes at the top of the cupboard the same size as a wine bottle cork and moderate the air flow by popping in and taking out corks as required.

4 *Hang in a cool location with good ventilation and out of reach of pests.*

5 *Or hang by a hook and air dry in a fridge over a tray to catch any drips.*

FLAVOUR GUIDE

Different materials produce different aromas and flavours when it comes to smoking, so it's important to consider both the food itself and the wood or other material you use in the smoker. The intensity of the smoke flavour is also important, and can be controlled not only by how much of the smoking material you use, but also how long you leave the food in the smoker.

For some foods, it's fun to overload the senses with a heavy, strong smoked flavour and really get a sense of the depth and aroma. For others, a more delicate approach is required, so the smokiness works in harmony with the other tastes rather than completely obliterating them. I like to try both approaches, so sometimes – for example for a slow-smoked pork belly

or brisket – I might use lots of hickory for that dense, bacon-like smoke hit, whereas for a good Cheddar I may want a more gentle applewood smoked flavour.

The table opposite is just a guide to food and smoke pairings – everyone has their own favourite combinations. The key is to select your wood to partner well with the food you want

Above left: **Mesquite wood chips, soaking.** *Above, top to bottom:* **alder chips, pine pellets and hickory.**

to smoke. There isn't a guidebook for experimenting with more unusual materials such as pine needles, liquorice root, juniper and manuka, so always feel free to be creative and come up with your own ideas.

Wood/Aromatic	Beef	Pork	Poultry	Game	Fish	Vegetables	Dairy	Description
Alder		🔥	🔥	🔥		🔥		Gives off only a little heat and has a subtle sweetness that enhances lighter meats. It's also good for fish that only needs a short cooking time.
Apple		🔥	🔥	🔥	🔥	🔥		One of my favourite smoking woods, applewood burns hot without much flame. It produces a mild and sweet smell and a fruity smoke flavour that is delicious with poultry and shellfish, but good with almost anything.
Citrus peel			🔥		🔥	🔥		This emits low heat and produces sweet, citrus smoke with a fruity flavour that is good with spices and sea-food, especially shellfish.
Cherry	🔥	🔥	🔥	🔥				Cherry burns hot with a low flame. It produces a slightly sweet and fragrant, fruity flavour that is great with pork and fruit.
Herbs and spices			🔥	🔥	🔥	🔥		These vary from spicy (bay, cinnamon, nutmeg, star anise) to sweet and delicate. Herbs with a higher oil content will provide stronger flavours, e.g rosemary and thyme.
Hickory	🔥	🔥	🔥	🔥		🔥	🔥	Burns slowly with a high heat and produces a strong smoky, robust, pungent, bacon-like flavour.
Maple		🔥	🔥		🔥	🔥	🔥	Burns rapidly with intense heat. Produces a mellow, smoky, sweet flavour.
Mesquite	🔥	🔥				🔥		Burns hot and creates a distinctive earthy, sweet flavour with vanilla notes.
Oak	🔥	🔥	🔥	🔥	🔥	🔥	🔥	Probably the best wood for all-round cooking, this is solid and slow burning and creates lots of heat and little flame. It produces a pleasant, dense smoke that blends well with wide range of flavours.
Pecan		🔥	🔥		🔥		🔥	This is good for low-heat smoking and has a rich, sub-tle character. It is milder than hickory but similar in flavour.
Seaweed				🔥	🔥			Creates a tangy, seafood, ozone flavour.
Tea				🔥	🔥			Imbues food with an aromatic, floral, dense smoky flavour.
Wine oak barrels	🔥	🔥				🔥	🔥	Produces an almost toasted coconut flavour and bold, dramatic charring.
Whiskey oak barrels	🔥	🔥				🔥	🔥	Provides an earthy, robust, peaty, toasted smokiness.

FLAVOURING FISH

Think of the smoke itself as another kind of seasoning; and as with any seasoning, it's easy to overdo it and overpower fish, which is generally more delicate than meat. Here's my favourite smoking materials for fish:

OAK – this classic bold flavour is great with mackerel and salmon, but easy to overdo

BEECH – the best all-round wood, this is light, subtle and fragrant and doesn't overpower the fish

APPLEWOOD – mild and fruity, a wonderful and reliable material for any fish or seafood

ALDER – salmon is often smoked with alder – a tradition that dates back to the indigenous peoples of the northwestern USA

TEA – this creates a really unusual rich, musky smoke and is often paired with mackerel and trout

TOOLS AND UTENSILS

Curing and smoking ideally requires some specialist equipment, which can improve the quality of what you achieve and how easily you can make certain recipes at home. However, most of the items can be stored in the kitchen and applied to your normal cooking and butchery, so they are sure to be put to good use.

If you are enthusiastic about curing and smoking then you will find that your toolkit will quickly grow, in which case my advice would be to store your equipment so it's easy to lay your hands on it. I keep my smoking and curing kit in a large case and enjoy the flexibility of being able to set up a field kitchen with everything together for easy access. It's also worth trying to make the most out of your vertical spaces, such as cupboards and sheds, to keep it all in good order.

If you invest in better-quality kit it is more likely to last longer, so I buy equipment that would be suitable for a professional kitchen, in the knowledge that it will last a lifetime and provide a great deal of pleasure downstream. Most of the tools are easily available online and, if in doubt, I'd suggest asking your local butcher for advice or visiting a charcuterie expert – who you might find at a farmers' market or food festival – and seeking their input.

TONGS

A long pair of tongs is a vital bit of kit for cooking on an open flame, not only to save sausages from falling between the grill and feeding the barbecue gods, but also for moving lit fuel and keeping the fire working.

HEATPROOF GLOVES

When you want to open or close a hot smoker, remove the grill to throw on some more smoking logs or handle hot cast-iron skillets, a pair of good-quality heatproof gloves or leather gauntlets is your best friend. I have found that welding gauntlets or fire gloves work well, but if you want more dexterity buy a professional pair from a barbecue supplier. Don't use oven gloves or a folded towel, they are not safe.

BLOWTORCH

In recent years, chefs have gone blowtorch crazy, with many items on the menu involving something being charred or singed. For me, though, while I may occasionally use a blowtorch for a bit of a theatrical finish on a garnish, primarily it's a practical tool I use to light the barbecue or start off a smoker.

Below: **For cooking with live flames you need to have tools with long handles to maintain a safe distance from the heat.**

Left: I have a selection of outdoor cooking boxes that I use for smoking. Cast iron skillets and variety of grill racks are worth having close to hand.

can be tricky to gauge the temperature accurately so it's helpful to be able to check the internal temperature and then adjust your heat source with some more lit charcoal or by tweaking the airflow. Having one also means you can check the temperature inside a smoker without having to open it up.

KNIVES

Investing in a good set of blades for different jobs provides endless satisfaction and a much smoother curing and smoking experience. I recommend the following knives:
BONING KNIFE – For cutting out bones from a pork belly or deboning a chicken, this knife is easy to move around meat and can transform what you achieve with your DIY butchery. They are sharp, narrow and flexible – perfect for crevices and carving out as much meat as possible.
SCIMITAR – A versatile scimitar is excellent for general butchery, raw meat prep and slicing. It is heavier than most knives and curved at the tip for a rocking chopping action.
MEAT CLEAVER – This is deal for vegetable prep but also for cutting through bone without causing it to splinter. A butcher's cleaver should be strong and relatively heavy.

SMOKER THERMOMETER

Smoking is all about temperature control, so you need good thermometers in your cooker and in your meat. Having an internal thermometer to see what level your heat source is burning at makes a big difference, but equally I like to use my hand and gauge the fire by simply feeling how hot it is. As ever, practice makes perfect and the more time you spend out with your smoker the more you will start to know what low, medium or high heat feels like. As a rule of thumb, holding your hand 15cm/6in from the grill should be comfortable for 5-6 seconds if the fire is generating low heat, 4 seconds for medium heat and no longer than 2 seconds if it's hot. If you're after a high temperature, you can try out a common test, which is that you should only just be able to say 'one Mississippi, two Mississippi' before having to move your hand if the temperature is right for hot smoking.

WIRELESS MEAT PROBE

Probing the internal temperature of your smoking and curing projects is a vital step, especially when you are learning the techniques. I use a meat probe as a safety guarantee; it helps provide peace of mind before you serve friends and families. Also, when you are cooking over an open fire, charcoal embers or barbecue grilling, it

Below: The temperature gauge on a smoker. Below left: A handy blowtorch. Below right: Digital meat thermometer.

CHEF'S KNIFE – Possessing an all-round chef's knife is a must in my eyes and you will find that it becomes key to your kitchen.

CARVING KNIFE – This isn't as necessary as the others for everyday use, but it certainly makes you look the part of an authentic pitmaster! A long, thin, slightly flexible blade that cuts long, even strokes perfectly, a slicer is perfect for brisket or salmon. Often they have a Granton (scalloped) edge to reduce sticking when cutting.

STEEL – Owning good knives is a big part of the puzzle, but keeping them sharp is what makes the real difference when preparing ingredients. I sharpen my knives very regularly – in fact, I often pause and sharpen the edge while working. Keep your steel dry and also explore getting a whetstone for certain blades that benefit from being worked up close.

MEAT-HANDLING MACHINERY

One of the key benefits of smoking and curing is that it is a relatively low-impact hobby that requires very little machinery. A traditional craft, it can be mastered with old-fashioned hand tools, but if you are keen on making your own burgers, sausages and salamis then it's worth thinking about buying yourself a meat mincer and sausage filler. There are hand-powered versions available for both, but electric ones will save you lots of energy and time and allow you to achieve more. I opted for a mincer-and-sausage-filler

Above left **Stainless steel knifes are worth the investment.** *Above right* **Syringes for brining mean you can also add flavour when cooking.**

combination machine that does the job for me. The key thing to look for is the option of grinding meat with different-width plates so that you can choose between coarse-, medium- or fine-grade mince.

TRAYS, BOXES AND BRINE TUBS

Given the range of curing methods, the volume of cures, brines and marinades

Left A table top mincer and sausage making machine can be expensive but provides hours of entertainment and they are extremely useful.

you need to work with and the need to safely store your produce at every stage, it is well worth investing in a range of plastic containers or bins. Avoid containers and equipment that could corrode or rust – it must be food safe – and I tend to not use glass as it's more expensive and heavy. Purchasing a selection of different sizes, ranging from small enough to cure bacon up to big enough to brine a whole ham or brisket, is a good move.

SYRINGE

Injecting brine and marinades deep into tissue when curing can help impart sweetness, keeps food moist and improves the preserving process. It also pumps in an extra depth of flavour.

BRINOMETER

As already discussed on page 14–15, a brinometer is a useful gadget for measuring the exact salinity of brine solutions, and a brinometer hydrometer can measure the percentage of salt in a solution at room temperature. They are readily available to buy online and are often sold by cheese-making stores.

STRING

When I visit my local butchers I tend to ask for some butcher's string when I've finished placing my order. It is food

Above Butcher's hooks are ideal for air drying pieces of meat or fish, and for hanging food in a cold smoker.

safe, easy to tie and durable – perfect for hanging meat and fish or tying up salami, as well as for rolling pancetta. An added benefit is that it doesn't dye the meat or brine since it isn't coloured.

MUSLIN

Wrapping meats in muslin is primarily something I do when I've finished the curing and smoking stages and want to preserve something by air drying. The muslin allows air to circulate around the products while still protecting them from pests and insects. If you are air drying outside you may want to consider building a drying box that can protect the food and still allow ventilation (see page 21).

HOOKS

I always make sure that I have a wide array of different shapes and sizes of butcher's hooks. They can be used in the fridge to optimise space and are very useful in smokers or to air dry food in a well-ventilated room.

WIRE BRUSH

I usually fire up my smoker for 15 minutes when I've finished cooking so that I can easily brush the grill clean. I also give the grill a good scrub with hot water and a stiff wire brush before I cook and while the smoker is coming up to temperature. It's good practice to adopt these cleaning rituals when working with fire so that your kit stays in good condition for longer.

Below A chimney firefighter makes life so much easier and means you can top up with extra heat for hot smoking.

HOME SMOKERS

Smokers come in all sorts of shapes and sizes and there is now a wide range available to buy ready-made to suit any budget. Alternatively, they can easily be built at home from scrap – old wooden cabinets, barrels, fridges or even a biscuit tin. I made my first cold smoker more than 20 years ago from an oil drum. It was very Heath Robinson (over-engineered) but it did the trick and served us well when we were learning the ropes. Since then, I've made a host of different smoking contraptions and even built a sandcastle smoker using a bucket, spade and a cardboard box. The principles remain the same and the requirements are fairly rudimentary, so be creative and have a go at making your own.

TYPES OF SMOKER

Fundamentally, there are two main types of smoker to consider: a cold smoker or a hot smoker. Whichever you use, you should always aim to cure your food first so that it takes on the smoke flavour properly.

COLD SMOKING – for which the ideal temperature is about 30°C/86°F – adds flavour and preserves food but doesn't cook it, so for smoked meat, poultry and some fish you need to then cook it. The exceptions are smoked salmon and trout, as well as fruit, vegetables and cheese, which can all be eaten straight from the cold smoker.

HOT SMOKING, on the other hand, cooks the food at the same time as smoking it, so you will need a heat source. This requires more management over the smoking period because you need to maintain an appropriate heat level. There are automated versions on the market, but I love the hands-on nature of hot smoking and dealing with fire. Despite being harder work than, say, putting on a batch of food to cold smoke and leaving it, the benefit is that you get to spend time near your smoker and

it feels more involved as a cooking process. You can opt for a smoker that is a hybrid of hot and cold and will do both jobs, although these tend to be more expensive. However, they are well worth the investment if you are serious about smoking food. At the other end of the scale, you can buy a smoking plank that you use just once or twice, which is a low-tech but very effective way of hot smoking foods.

There are also portable versions that allow you to hot smoke while camping, or in a standard kitchen environment on the stove, or even on board a boat when you go out fishing. I love having these in my shed because they give you the flexibility to enjoy smoked food wherever you are going. Take care when choosing one, though, since they vary in quality. From my experience, the more you spend the longer they last, and the better the end smoked product.

Kettle barbecue
I'd say that a kettle barbecue is an excellent way to start your smoking journey as it can be used for a lot of the methods in this book and many people already own one. Weber are without a doubt the market leaders for kettle barbecues; the design is flawless for both barbecuing and certain hot-

smoking techniques and they tend to be easy to manage and user-friendly. You can structure the Weber with hot coals on one side and place a foil tray to protect your food from too much direct heat on the other side, although the reality is that a kettle barbecue will often heat like an oven – with a well-distributed temperature – due to its shape. For this reason, I often use soaked wood chips to keep the smoke low and slow and avoid overpacking the charcoal, which will create fierce heat that is harder to manage; it is better to maintain a lower temperature with less charcoal and top it up as required with lit charcoal from a chimney starter during the smoking process.

Drum smokers
A drum smoker is similar to a kettle barbecue in some respects, although it offers more room and has an added shelf so that you can move your food around if required. The other benefit is that you can put in whole logs for a slower wood-fired smoke rather than just using wood chips. The downside is that they are heavy pieces of kit and less portable than a kettle barbecue.

I bought a Drumbecue smoker a few years ago and I use it for grilling, smoking and general outdoor cooking.

There are versions available with a bolt-on smoke box, but by managing where you put your heat source, adding smoking wood at the right time and keeping an eye on the air inlet, you can achieve a very good balance of heat and smoke without it.

Practice makes perfect and I have found that over the years my smoking has improved dramatically. The same goes for all smokers; they all present different challenges and are better for different jobs, which is why I like to have a collection of different types so that I can use them according to their strengths for a particular job.

Stove-top smokers
You can either make a small-scale hot smoker (see page 31) or buy a portable version. I own a few Cameron smokers that I use for cooking events, beach trips and in the kitchen. They are well made, simple to assemble, and very easy to clean. The benefit of a portable stove-top smoker is that you can make a small batch of smoked mackerel, for example, without firing up the larger smokers or barbecue. Some traditional smoking experts may question the place of quick hot smoking in the smoked-food scene, but for me it's accessible, fun and fits with family life. Sadly many of us are

short on time and as much as smoking food is a fantastic hobby, slotting it into a busy lifestyle can be difficult to achieve. The same can never be said about stove-top smoking, which is very quick and easy to do. If you fancy some smoked tomatoes with supper or a smoked avocado on toast, your set-up time is minimal. My only warning is that

you need to keep your kitchen well ventilated if you are smoking inside as I've been guilty of setting off my smoke alarm on several occasions...

Vertical stack smokers

Working with cold smoke often means setting up your smoker with fish or bacon hanging from a hook, or inserting grills laden with cheese at different heights. The real benefit of a vertical tiered smoker is that you have room to work with and they are easy to manoeuvre. I am a huge fan of the ProQ smokers because you can check the progress using small doors without disturbing the process. They also double up as hot smokers without needing any real modification.

Understanding the temperature inside your smoker is key, so the temperature gauge is a vital part of any commercial smoker. The other element to consider is adjustable airflow so that you can encourage draw or seal off the device for a dense smoke, depending on what is required. Modular designs also allow you to adapt the height, which means that you can keep it compact if you are smoking a small joint or expand it if you are smoking a whole side of salmon.

Open-fire smoking

This is one of the oldest smoking methods, and I still love to use it. The method involves hanging food above an open fire so it can be cold or hot smoked – you can slow cook a leg of lamb, pork shoulder or whole pineapples with hot smoke or you can cold smoke cured bacon, ham, sausages or kippers. My recommendation if you have an open-fire chimney is to put in a metal bar or some hooks and have a go! For cold smoking the heat must be less than 30°C/86°F. To assess this, you can put a thermometer at the back of the fireplace or use your hand; if it feels just warm then the temperature will be around the right mark for cold smoking, but if it is uncomfortably hot above the fire then allow the heat to die down or add some soaked wood chips. If the fire is very hot and you do want to hot smoke something, adding a large log to hot embers will often do the trick and generate a good smoky flavour as well as heat.

These are all just general rules of thumb, though; traditional wood-fired cooking and open-fire smoking is really another specialist subject in its own right. From Argentine *asado* to Australian beach barbies or Indian-style

Above **Smoking food in a chimney is basic but effective. Position the food high above the fire to avoid cooking.**

Above **A vertical stack smoker like the ProQ is ideal for hot or cold smoking. Its versatility makes it top of my list.**

Above **Cedar planks are cheap and accessible for smoking in the oven or a kettle BBQ, and are available online.**

tandoor ovens, all the methods from around the world come with a distinct set of trade secrets and deserve their own manual.

Grilling planks

Plank smoking is a basic, practical technique that's perfect for cooking all sorts of foods, but especially fish. Using wooden planks as a support means that you can open up delicate items to go into a hot smoker without risking them falling though the grill and feeding the barbecue gods. It can also impart a lovely secondary subtle smoky flavour from the plank itself. Any kind of food you would normally put in a hot smoker – meat, vegetables or fruits – can be cooked on a plank, but I only really use them for seafood.

Wooden grilling planks are normally about 15–30cm/6 x 12in in size, which are laden with food and go straight on to the grill or are propped up against a fire. They can be used a few times, but I tend to use them once and then break them up for kindling to start a fire. Don't use them in lump or chip form for smoking as some, such as cedar, may contain too much resin, which

SMOKE GUNS

Many purists think of smoke guns as cheating or not real smoking. However, as a chef in a professional kitchen I've used these out of choice because you can be very precise when adding subtle flavour to cured fish, delicate cheese or fruit, plus they are great for a bit of theatre and are really quick and easy to set up. To use one, first prime the smoke gun with some sawdust, tea or herbs in a pipe chamber with a fine gauze, then light the fuel. A battery-powered fan pulls the smoke through a pipe that you can feed under a cloche or into a sealed plastic container or zip-lock bag, gently smoking your food and imparting a subtle flavour rather than a deep smoked profile. NB, this method won't preserve your food. In my opinion, they are fun gadgets to own and worth experimenting with in order to appreciate the differences between different wood flavours and various smoke options before you go large with a big smoker. Think of them as a craft beer slider for a little taste before you commit and buy a proper pint...

can taint food. You can find planks online from stores that sell barbecue and smoking equipment. Going to an online retailer such as Amazon or ProQ (which specialises in grilling planks and other smoking accessories) will offer a good selection and allow you to buy them in bigger packs, saving you money. You can buy wood planks in a variety of different species – cedar, maple, oak, alder – each of which will impart different flavours; alder for a

gentler smoky flavour, while cedar brings a hearty, forest taste that works especially for a Pacific Northwest combination with salmon. You can get planks in differing sizes and grades, with fine, rough or medium grain, to allow more or less smoke to circulate off the surface and on to your food.

BENEFITS OF PLANK SMOKING
· Using a cedar plank gives your food a gentle smoky note that doesn't mask

HOW TO CREATE A HOT SMOKER

1 *Place a sheet of foil into the bottom of a large pan or casserole, then spread out some wood chips, tea, herbs or spices.*

2 *Position an upturned ramekin in the base and put a ceramic bowl containing the food to be smoked on top. Alternatively, position a wire rack on top if you are smoking, for instance, a fillet of fish.*

3 *Seal the smoker with a lid and then place it on a gas burner. Heat the pan until it starts smoking – it's as simple as that. Usually 10 minutes is plenty of time to hot smoke, but you may want to do it for longer for something larger, such as a duck breast.*

the delicate flavour of fish.

· It's easier to prime your smoker with wood chips if you use a plank, and it doesn't require as much preparation or time as other smoking methods. The risk with a lot of smoked food is that it dries out during the smoking process. Soaked planks, on the other hand, keep your food moist. It also has the added benefit of giving you more wriggle room when it comes to your smoking times, which can be extended a bit without overcooking the food.

· Using a plank means that your fish, vegetables or meat stays in one piece and doesn't fall through the holes in your grill.

· On occasions when you don't have time to set up your smoker outside or light the barbecue, you can also use planks for oven cooking food indoors, and still get a smoky quality without managing a fire.

HOW TO CREATE A HOT SMOKER

If you don't own a kettle barbecue or a drum smoker, both of which are usually ideal for hot smoking, then you can make a hot smoker at home using a large casserole dish, a wire rack and some foil.

The benefit of taking this approach to smoking is that you can have a go at home without investing in any specialist kit. The downside is that you often get quite a strong and dense smoke that makes food too intense. My advice is that less is more with regards to your wood chips, especially when you are starting out, so avoid using too many to start with.

As an alternative, you can take an old metal biscuit tin or bread bin and adapt it so that it has a wire rack suspended halfway up. This is good fun and perfect to take camping or on a road trip. That said, I like the adaptability, and lack of storage space required, of using a casserole and ramekin or wire rack – things that are already being

used in the kitchen and that can go back into general use once they have been cleaned.

HOW TO BUILD A COLD SMOKER

In their simplest form, cold smokers consist of a smoke chamber to hold the smoke and the food being smoked. Building one can be as easy as adapting a cardboard box so that it has a hole cut in the bottom as a door, a rack halfway up on which to put the food, and a hole in the top to encourage draw. If you want to upscale and build your own permanent structure, however, then a permanent smoke shack can be assembled from salvaged kit or custom-built.

Cold smoking food takes patience and practice so I find that it's more fun if you involve friends or family. The smoking community online is excellent for sharing top tips and helping with troubleshooting, so I'd recommend joining one and searching for advice online. That said, nothing beats the social element that comes from a gang of you constructing a smoker and then using it together, so it's worth turning it into a team effort.

Positioning the cold smoker

Locate your cold smoker somewhere near enough to the house so that you can check on it but away from windows and doors, and do be considerate of neighbours. If you have a garden shed then the smoker could be bolted on to that. Depending on how ambitious you are, you could even build your very own smoke shack.

Building a smoke shack

The base of the smoking chamber needs to be on a solid footing, which you can often construct using old materials. For ours, we created a solid base with some lime render before building a large box on top in which wire racking can easily be positioned. The cold-smoking chamber was not

constructed with treated wood as it's important to avoid using materials that may be coated in chemicals – if you are reusing old wooden cabinets or barrels make sure that you remove any paint that may taint your food and contain toxins.

For the firebox, we used firebricks and a pizza oven door, which means that we can add heat if we want to hot smoke. The key design aspects to consider are that you use a fireproof box or container, so that you can light the wood chips or sawdust with a blowtorch, and build the structure with a door to enable adjustable airflow. Keep the firebox relatively small to avoid the smoke escaping and locate it near to the main smoke chamber. You can use flexible ducting or flue pipe to connect the two elements together. Smoke then travels from the firebox along the pipe to the smoke chamber.

Other key design elements are a temperature probe to review the heat inside the chamber and an easy-access door for placing in and removing your smoked food. The scale of a cold smoker can be adapted to suit your space but I would also always consider additional storage room for a bin in which to keep sawdust dry. The temptation is to go large, but unless you plan on smoking huge quantities of food I'd advise keeping your build to a manageable size to reduce the costs and make it easy to light and operate.

Cold smoke generator

If you intend to light the cold smoker with sawdust, I recommend getting a cold smoke generator so you can achieve a perfect slow smoke (see page 13). This gadget produces a clean, cool smoke for up to 10 hours, works well in any sort of container or barbecue and can be placed straight into a single chamber or housed in a separate firebox. Light it with a tea light candle and, once it's smoking, that's it, you're all set.

BUILD YOUR OWN SMOKE SHACK

1 *Select a site for the smoke shack that isn't too far from the house but where sustained smoke won't be a problem.*

2 *The ground needs to be cleared, made flat. You might also need to clear some foliage away from the area.*

3 *Create a solid base with cement, or with sand and paving slabs or bricks. Make sure you extend it far enough.*

4 *Construct a simple wooden frame, with untreated wood.*

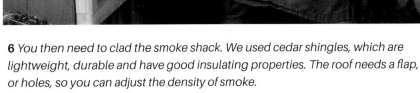

5 *Using heatproof materials, construct a small oven, connected to the smoke shack with a heatproof pipe.*

6 *You then need to clad the smoke shack. We used cedar shingles, which are lightweight, durable and have good insulating properties. The roof needs a flap, or holes, so you can adjust the density of smoke.*

If you don't have a cold smoke generator then arrange your sawdust in a coil formation and light it by positioning an empty can, half buried in sawdust, at one end. Make sure that your can has got plenty of holes drilled into the bottom, then using a blowtorch and the can as a channel to direct the flame, light the sawdust. Remove the can and leave the door open until the sawdust is smoking well; you are after smouldering rather than flames.

Another way to light your sawdust is to place a couple of hot coal embers on a small piece of newspaper and place on the sawdust. The downside of this technique is that you need to light the coals as well as the smoke generator.

COMMERCIAL SMOKERS

The popularity of smoked food and barbecuing has meant that many restaurants are reflecting the changing attitude with new menus that celebrate smoked meats and fish, and wood-fired kitchens are becoming more common. There is also a hugely successful street food and pop-up scene in the UK that has provided room for keen chefs to start up on their own and make a business out of their passion. If you are interested in purchasing a smoker for your restaurant, pub or bar, start selling your brisket on Saturdays, or if you just really love smoked food and want to take home cooking to the next level, then consider buying a commercial smoker.

SMOKER LOCATION

The first thing to consider when shopping for a commercial smoker is its eventual location. Fire safety laws and advice surrounding smokers in restaurants, festivals and public spaces vary. Some smokers are intended for stationary use only, while others are designed and equipped to be pulled on a trailer and moved at will. If you want to be flexible and take your smoker out on the road, say for a cooking demo or festival, then it makes sense to go for something mobile.

OUTDOOR SMOKERS

Most traditional smokers are intended for outdoor use and are designed with vents or chimneys for ventilation purposes. Commercial outdoor smokers vary drastically in size, so consider the volume of food you need to produce; if you are setting up to become a smokehouse selling smoked fish, for example, then you will need something very bespoke. Any restaurateur considering the

Above: **Ceramic stoves and smokers are very heavy so they are worth placing on a mobile frame.**

purchase of an outdoor smoker should consider the regulations and also the neighbours and the position of air vents. Conduct a full site survey before you get too carried away, and assess what is feasible. If you can make it work, the benefits of outdoor smokers are numerous: they're ideal for restaurants who want to attract customers keen to see some theatre with their food, and outdoor models are also typically much easier to set up and less expensive than indoor ones, since they don't require interior installation.

INDOOR SMOKERS

For many smaller restaurants that want to serve authentic barbecue food, the only viable option is an indoor smoker that's designed for commercial use. These typically require installation by an expert but there are solid options available off the shelf. If you aren't familiar with your new commercial smoker I strongly recommend saying yes to any training workshops that are offered, because each smoker has its foibles, and these can only be learned through experience.

Like outdoor smokers, indoor smokers can be found in many different configurations and sizes. Some are vertical, which is ideal for kitchens with small footprints, while others are squat and intended to be installed under a workspace. Before selecting an indoor smoker, take careful measurements of the space you have available, and make sure you have a comprehensive understanding of how the ventilation system will work.

CERAMIC SMOKERS

Made famous by Big Green Egg and Kamado Joe, these iconic pieces of kit are heavy-duty yet small enough to fit in a domestic garden, pub or small restaurant kitchen. They hold heat very consistently and can keep a good even temperature for cooking over long periods of time. You can use them like a tandoor, barbecue or grill. The ceramic plate that diffuses the internal heat for a low and slow oven is genius and they can be used indoors with a spark-protecting draft door for adjustable airflow. They tend to be quite expensive and they are not very portable., but they are very sturdy and super reliable for smoking in.

TENNESSEE SMOKER

This style of smoker has an offset barbecue, with a smaller chamber in which to burn the charcoal and wood.

Below, clockwise from top left: **A vent and thermometer are key for all smokers of this type. • Heat and smoke are kept at a good steady temperature by a good seal on the lid • Rotisserie accessories on smokers are a useful feature. • Ceramic smokers often have a grate to prevent embers escaping.**

Above: This large ProQ smoker is mostly aimed at restaurants and street food catering companies, or if you want to really impress your friends.

Above: The Bradley is an electric smoker that is used in many professional kitchens and is very reliable at delivering consistent results.

The airflow passes through a vent and cools in the main chamber. You can use it as a low-and-slow smoker that is perfect for briskets, ribs and pork shoulders. I also like the fact that it offers you the option to use the side firebox to keep charcoal hot and then top up the main chamber for hotter smoking and grilling. It's a very good system, and I think they epitomise the Southern pit-barbecue style for real authentic low-and-slow smoking.

BRADLEY SMOKER

The Bradley Smoker is an electric smoke house with an accompanying smoke generator in which flavour 'bisquettes' are burned for 20 minutes so that the temperature does not fluctuate. This not only gives consistent results, it also eliminates high-temperature gases, acids and resins that can distort the flavour of smoked food. Most smokers need to be tended to regularly, but the Bradley Smoker automatically produces clean, cool

smoke without intervention so it's good for a busy lifestyle or a kitchen that is focused on other things. The Bradley is capable of both hot and cold smoking, and makes clean-tasting food, but I have to say I would miss the element of raw creativity and fun.

BARBECUE TRAILERS

If you want to run a commercial barbecue with the ability to get out on tour and engage with the barbecue festival scene then an American-style commercial barbecue trailer could be perfect for you. They are practical,

BUDGET

Money don't buy you love, but it can buy you a better smoker. Generally, with commercial smoking equipment the more you spend the higher the quality of the equipment you will end up with. The only exception, in my opinion, is if you go down the route of a digital smoker with pre-made smoke briquettes. When it comes to electric smokers, I'd personally be wary of tying yourself into one supplier. Rather than the freedom of wood-fuelled commercial smokers and sourcing your own fuel, you can be trapped with a single brand and therefore miss out on the fun of being flexible with your recipes.

Another good option is to take the money you've set aside to purchase a commercial smoker or barbecue and commission, design and build your own bespoke one for a trailer or restaurant. This can really optimise your space and fuel your imagination to suit your own unique style. I like to have a mixture of commercial smokers available and some more DIY alternatives for when I want to be really creative.

*Above: **Pit Master style American smokers are excellent for festivals and catering events.***

reliably good smokers, and have a theatrical quality to them. Attending grill and barbecue events can be great for raising a business profile and is very profitable if done right. The sizeable main food chamber – often big enough for an entire pig – is ideal for large-volume event catering.

My only warning would be that in the UK our barbecue scene is still relatively seasonal and the commitment of working with a trailer on the road is hard. I ran a street food truck for a few years and the miles can take their toll. What's more, the footfall is hard to predict, which can lead to food-wastage issues if you misjudge it.

CABINET SMOKERS

Top of my personal wish list would be a ProQ cabinet smoker for events and a professional kitchen. The series of smokers from ProQ have been developed and designed to bring a viable solution to commercial barbecuing, while maintaining the

authenticity of cooking with real fire and smoke. With a wide range of features to ensure a reliable and sustainable alternative to electric or gas smokers, these beasts will give you the consistency and reliability required in a catering environment. The largest are gravity-fed with a capacity for around 80 racks of baby back ribs, or about 12–14 pork butts; this smoker is made for commercial use.

A lot of places use electric and gas smokers, but if you taste the product, you may notice something missing. There's no smoke ring, no bark and very little smoke flavour. Charcoal and real chunks of wood are the only way to get the authentic flavours that real barbecue needs. With the precise temperature control and consistency on the Gravity Feed Smoker series you can produce a better product with the same reliability.

A few smaller touches that I like are the built-in bottle opener (beer and barbecues go hand in hand, after

*Right: **Good for hot and cold smoking, quick to set up, and ideal for small catering events and at home.***

all), the extremely handy probe hole, the analogue thermometer, and the foldable table, which doubles as a Gastro (metal catering tray) holder or just a dry place to store a thermometer.

HOW TO SMOKE FOODS

Confidence and practice are key to managing your heat source when smoking food. It is important to get involved with the wood and coals and not to keep your distance and think that the fire will look after itself. Fire cooking is a living process that requires constant little adjustments; your tongs will become an extension of your arm for keeping the temperatures constant and the heat steady.

Don't be afraid of starting small and hot with how you build your fire, rather than going large and losing control of your heat source. The other thing to remember is that ultimately, once you get down to the embers, the deeper the layer of embers the hotter the smoker will be. I also try to stagger the rate of burn on my heat source, by putting some wood chips on hot coals and others on adjacent unlit charcoal to create a smoky Mexican wave, or chain reaction, that can keep smoking for hours.

FUEL STORAGE

Although damp charcoal will burn, it can be a nightmare to light. So, although you can in theory use the charcoal remaining in the firebox from your last cook, these coals may have absorbed moisture, particularly if it has been rainy or humid. To remedy

this, simply mix in 50 per cent extra dry charcoal to ensure faster lighting. Try to keep your spare charcoal in a dry environment or in a bin with a lid so it won't absorb humidity or moisture.

Despite taking these measures, though, depending on the time of year and humidity where you live, there will be changes to cooking times and the behaviour of your heat source. You need to be flexible and take it one flame at a time. I am never more relaxed than when I'm focusing on the task of working with a fire, aiming for a good constant temperature.

HOW TO USE A WOOD-FIRED SMOKER

Typically, a wood-fired smoker will be an offset smoker – i.e. the firebox is set to the side of the food chamber. Wood is fantastic fuel; even though I think it's probably the most difficult to control, there's something rustic about it. The heat is regulated by the intensity of your fire, which in turn is controlled by airflow through the smoker. Regulate this using the damper on the flue and the firebox.

I find that I normally have the flue damper fully open and that I regulate heat purely by controlling the firebox damper.

To get the fire going, I use kindling and an odourless fire lighter. In the first instance, open everything (dampers, doors lids) and get as much air to the fire as possible.

Your fire is ready when all of the exposed wood has charred and the initial thick white smoke has turned a wispy blue colour. You'll be hardly able to see the smoke and probably question whether this is right ... but it is, it's perfect. When you reach this stage you can batten down the hatches and start to regulate the temperature using the dampers. There must always be some airflow otherwise your fire will die and your smoke will turn stale.

HOW TO USE A CHARCOAL SMOKER

Smokers that use charcoal as a heat source come in all shapes and sizes but the principle remains the same: heat comes from the charcoal fire in the bottom of the smoker and smoke is

provided by wood chips dropped on to the fire. You may or may not choose to use a water bath. Personally, I prefer to use one as it increases humidity and so helps create a pink smoke ring on the meat.

To get your fire going, use an odourless fire-lighter cube, place some charcoal on top and open the bottom damper to get some airflow through the smoker. You need a decent fire but not such a raging one as you would have in a wood-fired offset smoker – just enough to heat the smoker. After that, it's about controlling the burn to give a steady flow of smoke from the wood chips and an even heat for the length of time you need.

Position your chosen type of wood chips on to the embers, putting some on the coals already burning and more on the unburned ones. That way you'll get a steady stream of smoke throughout the process. Some people will tell you to soak your wood chips prior to putting them on the fire but I usually don't bother unless I want to really delay the smoking for a longer and slower smoke, or if I don't have a water pan but do want some added moisture in the smoker.

GAS AND ELECTRIC SMOKERS

Using a gas-heated smoker is as simple as placing your wood chips on to the lava bricks or the ash pan and letting the chips smoulder. Electric heat sources employ a variety of systems: it could be the same as for gas ones – simply throw some wood chips on to smoulder – or your smoker could have a bisquette with an automatic feed or a pellet auger system. The latter uses wood pellets to provide both heat and smoke, and these are driven in a steady stream by an auger from a storage hopper to an electrically heated pan where the burn takes place. Whichever your smoker uses, you simply have to load the feeder and switch on the machine.

INDIRECT COOKING

Indirect cooking is achieved in a number of ways depending on the design of your smoker. Offset smokers have a firebox located to the side of the food chamber, while other smokers have the firebox directly under the food chamber and separate the heat source by either having the coals heaped to one side in the firebox or an ash pan. In the case of kamados such as Big Green Eggs) a ceramic plate is installed to diffuse the direct heat.

The benefit of indirect cooking is that it avoids flare-ups if the meat drips on the fire, which can cause water to douse the embers and fat to burn and produce dirty smoke that can taint the sweeter smoked flavours associated with a long, slow smoke.

For indirect cooking, you need to control the temperature across the grill. The easiest way to do this is to set it half and half – i.e. put all the coals or logs to one side, so you have a mega-hot side and one with no direct heat.

Then light the fuel, and during cooking only add hot embers. I set up a chimney starter (see page 44) nearby and use it to top up the fire when required. When it is burning properly, charcoal doesn't produce much smoke, so bear this in mind. Allow the fire to get rolling in your smoker and let the smoker warm up before you add any food, in the same way that you would preheat a conventional oven.

Plank smoking

Another method of indirect cooking, plank-smoked food needs a little longer to cook than if it were sitting directly on the rack, especially since the plank starts out wet. Before using a wooden plank, you must first soak it by submerging in water for at least 30 minutes with something heavy on top to stop it from floating. You could also soak in fruit juice or cider for something special, such as a large fillet of fish.

SLOW ROASTING

In addition to managing indirect cooking, one of the challenges of hot smoking is being able to cook for a long time at a relatively low temperature – typically 110°C/230°F to 125°C/257°F. It's this process that breaks down the tougher connective tissue in the meat, leaving you with that delicious juicy end result, but it can be

quite tricky to achieve – see below to find out how. You may find that during your initial smoking sessions you are constantly monitoring and tending to the temperature. This is normal and I find it great fun, and you'll soon get the hang of it as you gain in confidence.

CONTROLLING TEMPERATURE AND SMOKE LEVELS

Once you've lit your smoker you need to know how to control it. If your smoker has air vents, these can be used to regulate both temperature and smoke production.

Ensure that you keep the outlet – the vent located in a tall stack coming out of the top of the smoker – open to begin with as this promotes smoke 'turnover', allowing the smoke to escape and renew itself, which prevents overpowering, bitter flavours from forming. It also creates the draw that pulls air into the firebox.

The temperature in your smoker is directly affected by the volume of hot fuel and the amount of oxygen feeding it. When the bottom air vent is wide open, a large amount of air will be sucked in and will fuel the fire to the maximum of the smoker's capability, increasing both temperature and volume of smoke.

Closing the vent all the way will choke the fire of oxygen and eventually cause it to go out.

Position your smoker so that the bottom air vent is facing away from the wind direction so the wind will not penetrate the unit. This will help maintain an even temperature. To achieve a higher temperature, and particularly to increase the cooking temperature if it has dropped during your smoking session, you can carefully turn the entire smoker so that the bottom air vent is facing the wind direction. This will allow more oxygen into your charcoals, making them burn more quickly and increasing heat within the unit overall.

My standard process is to start with the bottom intake vent fully open to allow the heat to build. I then close it slightly if I want a longer, slower smoke. Keep your outlet vents open if you want a hotter smoker environment, and to allow smoke turnover, but partially close them if you are cold smoking and want to preserve food.

HOW TO USE A WATER PAN

Water pans are a feature of many hot smokers – if yours doesn't have one, you can just use a deep foil tray – and are something of a secret weapon when it comes to generating succulent smoked meats.

A water pan helps to provide a buffer between the food to be cooked and the heat source and therefore suppresses the heat, maintaining the required slow cooking temperatures. The water also infuses moisture into the sealed smoking chamber during cooking, and this ensures not only that your food never dries out, but also that it is cooked in moisture for extra succulence.

Fill the water pan or foil tray with hot (not boiling) water, as unlike cold water this will not interrupt the heat generated by the charcoal base.

For longer smoking sessions you may need to top up the water level during the smoking period.

The water pan can be perfumed with aromatic sprigs of herbs, such as rosemary, mint or bay. You can also try using cider or beer, although food science suggests that these flavours are unlikely to work their way into the food beyond glazing the surface. However, at the very least the scented water creates lovely aromas during the cooking process.

If you want to create hotter cooking temperatures and protect your food without using water, fill the water pan with sand. This will create a heat buffer without adding any additional flavour or moisture.

TYPES OF FUEL

Choosing what fuel to use for smoking your food is very similar to selecting a pan when cooking in the kitchen. Depending on the recipe and ingredients you may want a thick-bottomed pan for low and slow, a cast-iron skillet for a steady, even heat, or a shallow frying pan for intense high-temperature cooking. I make my decision about what fuel to use based on the time I have available to smoke the food and what flavours or seasoning I want to come off the wood so that it marries well with the dish.

Softwood

In general, softwoods such as pine, spruce or fir are evergreen conifers. The lower-density and highly flammable resins mean they burn more easily and quickly. Softwood can be very useful for lighting a fire but the resin exudes an acrid smoke and produces a bitter flavour that can destroy your smoked food. However, while I wouldn't recommend most for cooking, there are exceptions, such as cedar or juniper, which are lovely for light smoking on planks if they have been soaked in advance. You can also use dried pine needles, which burn intensely for a short period of time, to hot smoke mussels.

Hardwood

Most hardwoods are deciduous, and in the UK we have a good supply of oak, beech, cherry, birch, alder and apple. They tend to be slower-growing than softwoods and, as a result, they are denser with a more intense, sustained heat that is good for cooking with. Consider offering to pick up branches from a local orchard for some good fruitwood, and I also visit traditional boatbuilders, carpenters and furniture makers to ask for offcuts. Wood varies hugely from species to species and oak will burn very differently from something like chestnut. It is not an exact science but your fuel will have as much of an impact on your cooking as the ingredients you use. Experiment

WOOD

Considering what fuel to use is key when it comes to smoking food, and should be treated with the same care as seasoning with salt or spices. As a general rule, I like to use a blend of British lump wood charcoal for reliable fire management together with a hardwood to give more flavour to the

smoke and provide a more interactive vibe to the fire cooking. Cooking with fire and smoke is something that gets better the more experienced you are, so for me although charcoal briquettes have a place in smoking food, for the most part I'm drawn to the unpredictable magic you get from using wood in its natural form.

and try to source seasoned wood for the best results. You can also buy specialist wood for smoking – hickory wood chunks are available from many barbecue suppliers and whiskey oak barrels are becoming more popular in the UK.

SEASONED VERSUS GREEN WOOD

Whether you use seasoned wood or green wood makes a very big difference to the cooking process. Green wood is often still supple and contains much more moisture. Seasoned wood is dry, lighter, paler in colour and splits with a completely different cracking sound. It is referred to as seasoned because it has literally been left for a few seasons to dry out. Open-air seasoning is a maturing process for wood that is better than kiln drying it, and if you ask around you will find some excellent local suppliers. For something like oak you are talking about at least 2 years of seasoning for best results.

How to light a wood fire

1 To light a wood fire I like to use a log cabin method. Start by laying two logs parallel to each other, 30cm/12in apart, as the foundation.

2 Next, bridge these logs with two more parallel logs. This will help protect the fire from the wind but still allow airflow.
3 Lay four pieces of kindling across the logs and some tinder in the hollow. Then repeat, maintaining an open structure.
4 Light the tinder to set the cabin alight. Gently blow to encourage the flames.
5 You can also start a wood fire in a chimney starter. Fill the chimney with hardwood chunks and light as you would charcoal. Alternatively, light

some charcoal in a chimney starter and use it as an under-fire to bring the wood to flame.
6 Allow plenty of time – up to 45 minutes – for the fire to mature and burn down to embers. Then, with a shovel or long-handled grill, hoe rake the glowing orange embers underneath the grill grate. As with charcoal, the deeper the pile, the higher the heat.
7 Wood burns faster than either lump charcoal or charcoal briquettes. Be prepared to replenish the embers every 20–30 minutes.
8 Keep a fire extinguisher, water bucket or a pile of sand and a spade nearby to keep the fire from spreading out of control. Extinguish the fire completely once you have finished with it.

LUMP CHARCOAL

Hardwood lump charcoal is one of my favourite fuels to use for smoking as it provides a good plateau of heat and, although it doesn't burn uniformly like briquettes, it doesn't contain any additives, such as sawdust or petroleum, which can taint your food.

Today, the process of making lump charcoal typically begins with logs being stacked in underground pits and covered with sheet metal and earth.

The logs are lit at one end of the pile and the wood smoulders for a few days. During this time, the oxygen-starved fire burns off water, sap and other volatile substances in the wood. What's left is almost pure carbon, also known as char or lump charcoal.

Grilling and smoking food over a lump charcoal fire is an interactive experience. It gets very hot quickly, usually in less than 15 minutes, and the intense heat can sear food in seconds, browning the surface and scenting it with pure wood smoke aromas. In many cases, the smokiness emanates from one kind of wood only, such as mesquite or oak. Quite often, though, a bag of lump charcoal will hold a mix of hardwoods, including oak, hickory, maple and possibly some tropical woods from South America or Asia. For me, this is one of the downsides of cheaper lump charcoal – you can get a very mixed flavour, and the sourcing needs to be questioned. I opt for sustainably managed British charcoal, so I know the wood has not had anything to do with habitat degradation and deforestation.

Once a lump charcoal fire gets to its hottest point, it begins to lose heat rather quickly. In many cases the temperatures will fall from high

heat to medium heat in less than 30 minutes. This means that if you want to maintain a certain temperature range for cooking, the fire needs replenishing. Fortunately, lump charcoal lights and heats so quickly that you can get a burst of heat within 5–10 minutes by using your chimney starter or adding a few unlit coals. For a longer heat plateau I often put some oak logs on to a charcoal fire to boost the middle section of cooking time and maintain a stronger, steady heat source.

BINCHOTAN
Binchotan is the charcoal traditionally used for Japanese yakitori grilling. It is a type of lump charcoal, but one with very different characteristics to the common forms, being primarily made from holm oak. The tree clippings are stacked vertically in a large coil and charred at a low temperature for 2 weeks, before being heated at a high temperature until the smoke is clear and all the impurities have burned away. The result is nearly 100 per cent pure carbon, which burns steadily as a fuel. It exceeds other types of charcoal in its burning time of up to 5 hours and that it can be extinguished and started again up to three times. The downside is the cost, which can be high.

CHARCOAL BRIQUETTES
Briquettes are basically charcoal dust with a starch binder mixed up with additives, and it is claimed it releases a stronger heat for longer. Frankly, there's little in the heat strength argument but they certainly last longer and this is the important point – they give off a consistent level of heat. Other positives are that there's less ash and cleaning up is a little easier, and with practice, you can forecast when food will be ready and minimise fuel waste by using a certain quantity of briquettes with a fairly standard level of heat. Personally, I didn't get into smoking food to be accurate with timings and heat levels. I get my buzz from the organic interaction with the fire and nurturing the flames rather than sitting back and observing the process. Some chefs and smoking experts swear by them, though, so make up your own mind and give them a go.

SELF-LIGHTING CHARCOAL
Avoid this stuff, which comes wrapped up in a flammable brown paper bag that you place in the grill and light. It doesn't burn well, and is impregnated with fuel that will taint the flavour of your food. It also creates light ash, which can stick to your food.

BUYING AND PREPARING PRODUCE

When it comes to smoking and curing your own food, it is vital to start with good-quality meat and fish. I prefer to buy mine from a local butcher, farm shop or fishmonger to ensure I am getting a decent product that has been raised or caught in a sustainable way. An added benefit is that the butcher or fishmonger can probably offer their expert knowledge on the best-value cuts to cook with, and prepare it to your exact specifications if you choose not to do this yourself at home, although this is not as hard as it seems – read on to learn how.

MEAT, POULTRY AND GAME

I strongly recommend buying meat from a local farm or butcher in order to select local products as well as rare or native breeds that mature naturally, the slower development of which results in a superior flavour. Selecting the right meat can often be confusing for curing or smoking novices and my advice would be to talk to your butcher to get

their advice. Although you could justify buying cheap plastic-wrapped meat from the supermarket for learning the ropes, but your end product will not taste as good as one that has been made with responsibly raised, high welfare meat that has had longer to mature, so it's worth spending a little time and money on the product. Once an animal has been slaughtered, the

next step is butchering: cutting the carcass into smaller and more easily handled parts. Beef, lamb and pork are all broken down into basic cuts called primals; beef into eight primals, and lamb and pork into four. The next steps are cutting and trimming, and preparing for cooking or smoking. The cutting stage is hugely varied and a really specialist area; you can cut into

Like the art of smoking food, practice makes perfect when it comes to knife skills, and attending a specialist course or day workshop, or watching videos online, can help to give you some hands-on experience and tuition before attempting all of the recipes and methods in this book. Personally, I have found that the key to good knife work is to constantly sharpen your blades with a steel or whetstone, working at least 25 degrees down the step and applying only gentle pressure. Also, store your knives on a wall magnet or in a pouch, not in a drawer, where they can easily go blunt. I also have my own knives at home for butchery and another set for general family use to avoid anyone accidentally putting the former in the dishwasher or not treating them carefully. One of the secrets to domestic bliss is, strangely, not sharing your knives!

cubes for stews, grind for burgers, finely grind for pâté, thinly slice for jerky or slice between the bones for ribs.

Cutting boards

The best surface for cutting meat is a close-grained wooden board. An end-grain board or butcher's block is easy to clean and will help your knives stay sharper for longer. Newer plastic boards are also good because they are easy to clean, but older ones that bear knife scars should be replaced. Wash all boards in hot soapy water after use and, if possible, keep a separate board for meat and poultry.

Beef

Our British beef heritage is something to be proud of and there has been a resurgence of traditional breeds in recent times. Longhorns have never been exported so remain totally British and there are many other top-quality grass-fed breeds, such as Herefords, Red Devons, Belted Galloways and Aberdeen Angus available if you want something special. Sadly, however, most of the beef consumed in the UK now comes from the dairy breeds, mostly Holstein Friesian cows. There is also a growing rose veal scene that it worth exploring, but generally the majority of beef is leaner and less muscular than it would have been historically.

AGED BEEF Well-hung beef should appear dry on the outside, soft to touch and hold a thumb's imprint when pushed in for a few seconds. Dark red in colour on the outside, when it is cut open the inside will appear a lovely bright red and have a gamey smell. Also look out for good levels of fat marbling, which will help it to stay juicy.

BEEF CUTS
For smoking and curing I tend to primarily use the following cuts of beef: Brisket – Wrapped in fat, this is a classic cut for salting and slow smoking. It comes from the lower shoulder and will remain lovely and moist when hot smoked.

- Jacob's ladder/short ribs – These big juicy ribs are becoming increasingly popular and are beautiful slow smoked on the barbecue.
- Silverside – This part of the rump is lovely for making salt beef and is also good for jerky.
- Flank steak – I like to cut across the grain and slice this thinly for jerky.
- Oxtail – If you can slow roast this with smoke and then add it to a casserole, you will be in for a treat; it's a tender meat packed with flavour.

- Fore rib – The layer of fat bastes the meat and makes it succulent. The ribs from the upper part of the back are best cooked on the bone over smoke.

Pork

I started rearing pigs of my own around 10 years ago, so I know from experience that rare-breed pigs are a joy to look after and a pleasure to eat. However, some of the old-fashioned breeds, such as Cornish Black or Gloucester Old Spot, can carry excessive amounts of fat. By contrast, cross-breeds such as a British Lop and Large White create strong, healthy animals and the fat layer is perfect for making rustic bacon and sausages. When compared to mass-produced breeds I think there is no competition; commercial pig farmers select breeds with less fat that are fast-growing and bear big litters. This makes them more profitable but they are often confined in indoor pens and, for me, the questionable welfare is a serious issue. Free-range pigs, by contrast, have a much better life and will produce meat that is packed with flavour, moistness and far fewer antibiotics. Good pork will be easy to spot; it's firm to touch, rosy pink in colour and there's no excess moisture from being injected or soaked in water.

PORK CUTS

For smoking and curing I tend to primarily use the following cuts of pork:
- Shoulder – Whole or boned and often slow smoked, this juicy cut is big and so ideally suited to large gatherings. It can also be diced and minced for sausages.
- Spare ribs – Cut from the upper part of the shoulder, the generous amount

of marbled fat on ribs means that they are perfect on the grill or in a hot smoker. They are especially delicious coated with a barbecue rub and slow smoked with water in a pan to keep them succulent and moist.

· Belly – This cut is ideal for sticky burnt ends or for curing and smoking your own bacon. The thick end comes from nearer the shoulder. You can slow roast belly whole with the bones or remove them with a boning knife.

· Back bacon – The long back bacon joint stretches from the middle of the back down to the belly bacon so you get both eye and streaky in one cut.

· Leg – The classic king of cured meats, hams can be broken down to be smaller or rolled for a roast. A good-quality leg of pork should have enough fat marbling to remain moist when it is brined and smoked.

Poultry

Factory-farmed poultry and the appalling welfare conditions of caged chickens have had plenty of publicity in recent years, and nowadays most people choose to buy free-range eggs. I also always only buy free-range birds for meat, as not only do they offer so much more flavour, but you also avoid supporting sub-standard farming practices. More slowly matured chickens take longer to develop but aren't packed with the antibiotics and additives given to lower-welfare birds to make them put on weight rapidly.

CHICKEN CUTS

For smoking and curing, I tend to primarily use the following cuts of chicken:

· Breast – This lean white meat has a milky taste and can be barbecued or

cured to good effect. Cold-smoked chicken breast can be very delicate in flavour – a real treat.

· Thigh – Moist and dark, thigh is good on the barbecue, for confit, or grilled.
· Drumstick – Flavoursome and slightly chewy, this is lovely hot smoked.
· Wing – This brown meat is best marinated and smoked before being eaten with fingers and a good barbecue sauce.
· Parson's nose – This meat is very tender and makes a great option on yakitori skewers for a charcoal-smoked delicacy.

Game

The commercial growth of bred and hatched game shooting means that there is now often a very large supply of birds available at certain times during the game season. If you want to find a local source then I'd suggest going to a smaller farm where wild game is shot, or finding a local supplier or game merchant.

Pheasant is the most popular game bird in the UK and is often very good value between October and February. Check with your butcher that the bird has already been hung.

Rabbit is readily available and can be delicious when slowly smoked. Avoid farmed rabbit as the quality of meat is far inferior – instead try to find a supply of wild rabbit.

Venison is available from August to February and this lean meat is ideal for jerky or sausages and salami. Farmed deer is available all year round and is generally always free-range, so ethically it's a good meat to source.

SEAFOOD

Living near the sea in Cornwall, we are lucky to have a host of good local fishmongers and fish merchants selling fresh fish, and I have grown up smoking and curing lots of local seafood. These processes can add flavour and, if done correctly, preserve seafood for longer, although you must start with a good-quality product before attempting the recipes and methods in this manual.

Choosing fresh fish

If you are smoking or curing your own fish then you must start with the freshest produce. Here are a few things to consider when you visit the fishmonger:

· Skin – A good fresh fish should look shiny and alive with moist skin. The

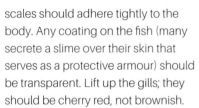

- Keep all live seafood, such as crabs, mussels or oysters, at 4.4°C/40°F. You want to keep them alive, so surround them in seaweed, damp newspaper or sea grass to insulate them so they don't get too cold, which will kill them.
- For non-live seafood, by contrast, keep it buried in ice if possible.
- Never eat dead shellfish. Only consume shellfish that has unbroken, tightly closed shells before cooking.
- Avoid cross-contamination by using a separate washable cutting board and keeping raw seafood juice away from other foods.
- Avoid certain types of fish and shellfish if you are pregnant – check the latest official guidelines.

scales should adhere tightly to the body. Any coating on the fish (many secrete a slime over their skin that serves as a protective armour) should be transparent. Lift up the gills; they should be cherry red, not brownish.

- Flesh – You want this to be firm to the touch; when pressed it should be taut enough to spring back without a depression being left in the surface. The grain of the flesh should be dense without gaps between the layers, and if the fish is pre-wrapped in plastic be sure there is no liquid leaking, since this is a sign of age.
- Smell – Trust your nose. The fish should smell briny and like the sea or for a freshwater fish clean with no muddy or ammonia aroma.
- Eyes and tail – Eyes should be clear and protruding and the tail should be moist and flat, not dried up or curled.

How to fillet fish

If you are planning to cure or smoke a smaller fish, such as sardines, then filleting is a method that works well and doesn't involve any gutting.

1 To begin, lay the fish on a clean cutting board with its backbone towards you and its head in your hand.

2 Make a deep diagonal cut behind the gill, angling the knife towards the front of the fish to reach the flesh behind the skull. Using a thin and flexible knife, cut back down the spine with a flat blade

level to the table to remove the first fillet. Stop at the tail. You should now have sliced the fillet cleanly from the bones.

3 For the second fillet, turn the fish over and make a diagonal cut behind the gill. Use the flat palm of your hand to guide the cut down the backbone to remove the second fillet.

4 Use the bones and the rest of the fish for making stock.

Below: Oily fish, like mackerel, are perfect for smoking.

How to butterfly fish

This technique is especially useful for preparing mackerel and herrings before smoking them.

1 Place the fish belly down on a board, then slice down the backbone from head to tail using a thin and flexible blade. Don't go all the way through; you don't want to puncture the stomach and guts.

2 Use scissors to remove the spine, rib cage and viscera.

3 Clean out the cavity by rinsing the fish under cold water and patting it dry.

MEAT

There are few things in life that provide the luxury of living completely in the moment, finding a simple focus and doing one thing at a time. For me smoking meat does just that. The process involves some preparation, an understanding of the key skills and attention to detail, but when you settle in for a long, slow smoking session the world and your day-to-day worries fade away. You are left with a few almost instinctive elements to watch. When you find your rhythm with the recipes and methods in this manual, you'll start to enjoy the whole act of smoking meat as some sort of relaxing ritual. If you find yourself worrying too much or stressing about the food, then you've got it all wrong. Of course good hygiene and food safety are very important, but beyond the basics of cleanliness, my advice is to remember to enjoy the ride.

CONFIDENCE

Smoking meat really is relatively easy for beginners to master, so don't be intimidated. I must confess that I used to have my own brisket inferiority complex, born out of looking at so many photos on Instagram in which blokes proudly showed off the depth of their smoke ring and barked about the brisket as though their way was the only way. It's cool to be proud of your creations, but remember that making food at home isn't about comparing yourself with the professionals; it's for the enjoyment of you, your friends and family. Also, never be afraid to break the rules and try something new and out-of-the-box, such as an unusual combination of hickory and liquorice with duck, or a horseradish barbecue rub on your Sunday beef. Write your own recipes and be creative.

LOW 'N' SLOW

Smoking meat can't be rushed. As a rule, for most recipes you are looking at 4 hours or more, so dedicate some time to it. Meat that's going into the smoker is a long-term investment with significant pay-offs. Be patient and remember that when smoking several items you really need to set aside the whole day. Key phrases are 'slow and steady', 'low and slow' and 'take your time'... These are fundamental to smoking, and although I'm sure you could try fitting it into a busy weekend, I fear you'd miss out on reaping the rewards of the act itself, which is to slow down and live in the moment.

Good things come to those who wait, so avoid peeking or checking on your meat too often and don't move it around if you are cooking slowly on indirect heat. Flipping and turning is generally unnecessary, and opening the smoker to check on progress will dissipate the smoke and cause cooking temperatures to fluctuate. There are exceptions, such as when you need to top up your smoker with hot coals and refill your water pan to keep meat moist, but on the whole the best rule to follow is only open your smoker when you have to.

SOURCE GOOD MEAT

The more you can afford to spend on locally reared, high welfare meat, traditional breeds rather than intensively reared animals, the tastier your dishes will be. In my opinion, an animal that has put on good natural fat levels, matured slowly and been slaughtered without stress, tastes a million times better than a cheaper factory-farmed joint of meat pumped full of water, growth hormones and antibiotics.

The cuts themselves certainly don't need to be expensive prime ones. In fact, actively avoid choosing to smoke more expensive, leaner meat such as pork tenderloin or fillet steak, as these are far better for grilling. It's worth asking your butcher what they've got available that is good value, well marbled and would suit low-and-slow cooking.

GO SUPERSIZE

If you can smoke ribs or a joint of belly pork, you can probably have a go at a whole hog. The principles are the same and it comes down to confidence and practice. I've often gone straight in at the deep end and although to a degree it's sink or swim time, more often than not you'll be pleasantly surprised at how successful your efforts might be. If you have the beginner's guide nailed, then you can take on any pitmaster. Be ambitious and give it a go!

WET OR DRY?

Adding moisture into a smoker with a water pan can create a steamy smoking atmosphere that helps keep meat moist. Some people believe in using cider, beer or fruit juice for added flavour but the science clearly indicates that this doesn't actually penetrate the meat and may just make the cooking process smell better for the attending chef. The downside to using water in a hot smoker is that your meat will develop less bark or smoky crust, and if the water all evaporates off then the temperature can increase and cause overheating.

PRESENTATION

Having spent a long time smoking meat, I've come to realise it's a good idea to take a moment when you are ready to serve. Think about plating it on a larger sharing platter, finishing it with a glaze, or perhaps carving the meat at the table for some dining interaction. You could even go so far as to share the experience with your guests and get one of your friends or family to help pull your pork shoulder at the table, carve the smoked turkey or slice the brisket. I find that the short moments before you eat are the most intense and mouth-watering seconds of the whole smoking-meat experience, so rather than proudly parading the food to the table as a magnanimous gift, get your loved ones involved at that exciting point and forget the old idea of 'chef's perks' enjoyed in private – dig in together.

SMOKED PORK SHOULDER

serves: 6-8
difficulty: 🔥🔥
wood: mesquite
equipment: large zip-lock bag, bowl or container, hot smoker, brush
marinating time: 1-12 hours
smoking time: 4 hours
target temperature: 150°C/300°F

30ml/2 tbsp molasses
50ml/2fl oz/¼ cup water
50ml/2fl oz/¼ cup soy sauce
15ml/1 tbsp coconut flakes
15ml/1 tbsp sea salt
1 habañero chilli, finely sliced
1 small onion, finely diced
5ml/1 tsp fennel seeds
5ml/1 tsp coriander seeds
5ml/1 tsp yellow mustard seeds
1kg/2¼lb pork shoulder

For the mop:
150ml/¼ pint/⅔ cup golden rum
100ml/3½ fl oz/½ cup chicken stock
100ml/3½fl oz/½ cup pineapple juice
30ml/2 tbsp soy sauce
30ml/2 tbsp molasses
2 spring onions (scallions), thinly sliced
4 garlic cloves, crushed
50g/2oz¼ cup butter, melted
30ml/2 tbsp chopped fresh coriander

The Hawaiian way of cooking pork is a celebration of low and slow, often underground in a traditional kalua. This is my take on the technique that captures the tropical flavour, using first a flavour-packed marinade and then a sweet spiced rum mop that is brushed on the pork shoulder as it smokes. Smoky pineapple and a zing of lime finish the dish.

1 Make a marinade by mixing together the molasses, water, soy sauce, coconut flakes, salt, chilli, diced onion and spices.
2 Rub the pork all over with the mixture, place in a large zip-lock bag, bowl or container and leave to marinate for an hour or overnight.
3 Set a fire in a hot smoker and preheat it to the target temperature, then prime it with some mesquite chips.
4 Mix together all the mop ingredients.
5 Place the shoulder in the smoker and slow smoke it for 4 hours, brushing it with the mop after an hour of cooking and then repeating every 45 minutes. For the last hour of cooking, cover the shoulder with foil, to keep it moist.

TIKI SMOKED PORK SHOULDER WITH PINEAPPLE

serves: 6-8
difficulty: 🔥🔥
equipment: 2 large forks (optional)
grilling or roasting time: 30-45 minutes
steaming time: 3-4 minutes

smoked pork shoulder
2 pineapples
bao buns
spring onions (scallions), finely sliced
6 limes, quartered

1 Peel the pineapples but leave them whole, then either grill them on the barbecue or hang them over an open fire until charred and tender. Dice to create a sweet and smoky salsa.
2 Remove the crackling from the smoked pork and pull the meat into shreds and chunks using two large forks or your hands. Add extra mop to keep it all moist.
3 Steam the buns for 3-4 minutes, then layer in the smoked pulled pork shoulder, some finely sliced spring onions and the pineapple salsa. Garnish with lime wedges, for squeezing over.

SMOKED BRINED GAMMON

Making your own ham from scratch gives you the flexibility to add real some flavour and in my opinion there's nothing more satisfying to carve and serve. This brining recipe uses a sweet cure and I glaze the ham with something a bit different for a barbecue twist – Dr Pepper and orange juice is a special combination that really works with mustard and cloves.

serves: 8
difficulty: 🔥🔥🔥
wood: maple
equipment: brining tub, kitchen paper, large pan, hot smoker, knife, small pan, brush
brining time: 2-3 days
cooking time: 4 hours
target temperature: 180°C/350°C

1kg/2¹/₄lb gammon joint
30-45ml/2-3 tbsp cloves
baked potatoes and steamed cabbage, to serve

For the brine:

500g/1¹/₄lb/2¹/₂ cups salt
750g/1lb 10oz/3³/₄ cups sugar
5 litres/8³/₄ pints warm water
2-3 bay leaves
5ml/1 tsp black peppercorns
2 star anise
4 cloves
1 cinnamon stick

For the glaze:

150ml/¹/₄ pint/²/₃ cup Dr Pepper or other cola
75ml/5 tbsp orange juice
30ml/2 tbsp soft light brown sugar
15ml/1 tbsp Dijon mustard

1 Dissolve the salt and sugar in the warm water in a brining tub, then add the aromatics and leave to cool. Submerge the gammon in the sweet brine, cover and leave, chilled, for 2-3 days.

2 Lift the gammon out of the brine and pat dry with kitchen paper, then submerge it in a large pan of cold water. Bring to a low simmer then cook for 3 hours. To avoid your gammon tasting too salty, after the first hour of cooking pour away half the water and top up with fresh boiling water.

3 Remove the gammon from the pan when the fat starts to separate from the meat, and allow to cool slightly.

4 Set a fire in your hot smoker, preheat it to the target temperature, and prime it with some maple chips.

5 Remove the skin from the gammon, leaving as much fat as possible. Score the fat with a diamond pattern and place a clove in the middle of each diamond.

6 Put the glaze ingredients in a pan and bring to a boil, then cook for 10-15 minutes, until the glaze starts to thicken. Brush on to the ham generously.

7 Hot smoke the ham for about 45 minutes, basting occasionally with the glaze, until it's caramelised and smoky.

8 Plate up thick, warm slices with baked potatoes and some steamed cabbage.

THREE WAYS WITH PORK BELLY

Curing pork belly can produce three different products: dry-cured bacon, smoked dry-cured bacon and pancetta. All start with the same recipe and process, which takes some time and planning, so I tend to try to work ahead of myself and to have cuts of bacon ready at different stages – some in the fridge curing while other joints are air drying. Once the belly is cured you can cook the bacon as it is, cold smoke it to add depth of flavour, or leave it to air dry with some of the cure left on to make Italian-style pancetta. All need to then be sliced and diced and cooked before they are eaten.

makes: 1kg/2¼lb
difficulty: 🔥🔥🔥
wood: mesquite
equipment: 2 large airtight containers or zip-lock bags, kitchen paper, muslin, butcher's twine, hook, cold smoker, clear film (plastic wrap), heavy meat tenderiser, rubber mallet or rolling pin
curing time: dry-cured and smoked bacon 5 days; pancetta 5–7 days
air drying time: smoked bacon 2 days; pancetta 2 weeks
smoking time: smoked bacon 6–8 hours
target temperature: For curing 5°C/41°F, for air drying 15°C/60°F

1kg/2¼lb pork belly middle bacon

For the cure:

500g/1¼lb/2½ cups salt
500g/1¼lb/2½ cups soft light brown sugar
30ml/2 tbsp juniper berries, crushed
15ml/1 tbsp cracked pink peppercorns
10ml/2 tsp chilli flakes

DRY-CURED BACON

1 Mix the cure ingredients together in a large airtight container or zip-lock bag and keep any you aren't using in the fridge.

2 Start by rubbing 100g/3¾oz of the cure into the pork meat, using one-quarter of the mixture on the fat side and the rest on the meat. Put the pork in another large airtight container or a zip-lock bag (I use the fridge's base salad box) and store in your fridge for 24 hours.

3 The next day pour off any water that has been drawn out off the meat and top up with another 100g/3¾oz of your cure. Repeat this process for 5 days in total. Your bacon will firm up and darken slightly in colour. After dry curing you will need to rinse it in a little water.

4 Pat dry with kitchen paper, then wrap it in muslin, securing it with butcher's twine, and hang it in a cool place for 5 days (see page 20–21).

5 When you want to eat it, slice the bacon into rashers (strips) or dice it into lardons, then fry or grill (broil) it. Store in the fridge.

SMOKED BACON

1. Follow the method for dry-cured bacon up to the end of step 5, then leave it to air dry in a well-ventilated, cool place for 2 days.
2. When you are ready, prepare your cold smoker (see page 32) and prime it with some mesquite chips.
3. Place the dry-cured bacon in the smoker, close the lid or door and leave the bacon for 6–8 hours.
4. Once it is ready, slice the bacon into rashers or dice it into lardons, then fry or grill it.

PANCETTA

1. Follow the method for dry-cured bacon up to the end of step 3, curing it in the fridge for a total of 5–7 days.
2. Remove the dry-cured belly (pancetta) from the fridge and let it sit at room temperature for about 3 hours, until it is soft and malleable.
3. Cover a large cutting board with clear film and lay the pancetta, meat side up, on top. Place another layer of cling film on top.
4. Using a heavy meat tenderiser, rubber mallet or rolling pin, pound the pancetta thoroughly, evenly, and without mercy for a full 5 minutes, until it is more pliable and easy to roll.
5. To roll and tie the pancetta, lay the belly, meat side up, with its longest side closest to you. Fold the first 5cm (2in) of the side closest to you over on to itself and press down firmly. Continue to roll and press, making sure you eliminate any air gaps, which can result in mould on the inside of the pancetta.
6. When the belly is completely rolled, tie it as tightly as possible with butcher's twine, as you would a roast, then hang it in the fridge for another 2 weeks or until it is firm to your liking.
7. Untie the string and unroll before slicing it into rashers or lardons for frying.

SMOKEHOUSE BLT (BACON, LOBSTER AND TOMATO)

serves: 4
difficulty: 🔥🔥🔥
wood: lump charcoal
equipment: 2 small pans, frying pan, knife, food processor or blender, butter paper or clear film (plastic wrap), brush, blowtorch (optional)
cooking time: about 10 minutes

115g/4oz/½ cup salted butter, melted
15ml/1 tbsp dried seaweed flakes
150g/5oz smoked streaky (fatty) bacon
115g/4oz heritage cherry tomatoes
2 lobster tails, butterflied
6 scallops, in the shell
1 chorizo sausage (optional)
4 slices of sourdough bread, toasted
salt and ground black pepper, to taste
courgette (zucchini) flowers, to garnish
   (if you have them)

For the hollandaise sauce :

250g/9oz/1¼ cups salted butter, diced
5 egg yolks
1 garlic clove, crushed
2.5ml/½ tsp Dijon mustard
15ml/1 tbsp orange juice
5ml/1 tsp dried seaweed flakes
15ml/1 tbsp hot water (optional)

For the fennel salad:

15ml/1 tbsp grated orange zest
15ml/1 tbsp orange juice
15ml/1 tbsp finely chopped fresh basil
5ml/1 tsp olive oil
pinch of salt
50g/2oz fennel bulb, shaved or thinly
   sliced

If you are looking for a special surf 'n' turf dish that shows off your home-smoked bacon, then this luxury brunch idea is a real crowd-pleaser. Featuring butter-grilled lobster tails and succulent scallops cooked directly on hot coals, this open sandwich is finished with crispy home-smoked bacon, a generous dollop of seaweed hollandaise sauce and some citrusy, aromatic basil that balances it all perfectly. You can substitute the lobster for a smoked haddock fillet for another hot surf 'n' turf sandwich classic.

1. Prepare and light a charcoal fire pit or barbecue, you need quite a large surface area. It is ready when the coals are glowing and are covered in white ash.
2. Meanwhile, make a simple seaweed butter by melting the butter in a small pan over a low heat with the seaweed flakes. Set aside.
3. Next, fry your smoked bacon rashers until crispy, remove from the pan and break or chop into shards.
4. In the same pan, fry the cherry tomatoes until soft and juicy. Return the bacon to the frying pan and keep everything warm.
5. For the hollandaise, gently melt the diced butter in a small pan, then remove from the heat. Blitz the egg yolks, crushed garlic and Dijon mustard in a food processor or blender until smooth, then gradually pour in the melted butter, with the processor or blender still running. Keep adding butter until the sauce is smooth and silky, then stir in the orange juice and seaweed flakes.
6. Pour the hollandaise into a jug, cover with butter paper or clear film to prevent a skin from forming, and keep in a warm place. If you need to slacken the texture for serving, stir in a tablespoon of hot water.
7. For the salad, mix together the orange zest and juice, chopped basil, oil and salt, then pour the dressing over the fennel and toss well.
8. Grill the butterflied lobster tails and the scallops on the barbecue for 6–8 minutes, basting in the seaweed butter as they cook. Add thin slices of chorizo sausage to the shells if you want to add a hit of warming spice to the dish.
9. Once cooked, remove the shells from the coals, extract the flesh and place on toasted sourdough with the fennel salad, bacon and tomatoes and topped with hollandaise. Season to taste. Torch the hollandaise until golden and bubbling, if you like, and garnish with courgette flowers if you have some.

PANCETTA WITH PUMPKIN GNOCCHI

The chilli-spiked cure I used for my pancetta recipe (see page 61) works really well with these fluffy gnocchi and the salty anchovy. The kale adds some rustic metallic notes and the pumpkin and sage pesto gives it a sweet, nutty finish. Delicious.

serves: 4
difficulty: 🔥🔥🔥
equipment: peeler, knife, 2 large pans, metal sieve or potato ricer, large bowl, knife, fork, mortar and pestle or food processor, frying pan, kitchen paper, colander
cooking time: 30 minutes

150g/5oz pancetta, diced
115g/4oz kale
4 sage leaves
grated Parmesan, to serve

For the gnocchi:
750g/1lb 11oz butternut squash
300g/11oz/2½ cups 00 flour, plus extra for dusting
2 egg yolks
pinch of salt

For the pesto:
12 sage leaves
15ml/1 tbsp pumpkin seeds
pinch of salt
6-12 anchovies
50g/2oz/²/₃ cup grated Parmesan
15ml/1 tbsp olive oil

1 For the gnocchi, peel and roughly chop the butternut squash, then boil it in a large pan of water for 15-20 minutes, until soft.

2 Push the squash through a metal sieve or a potato ricer into a large bowl, to make a smooth purée. Allow to cool.

3 Mix in the flour, then beat in the egg yolks and a pinch of salt until it forms a dough. Knead to ensure it is smooth.

4 Roll the dough into a long, thin sausage on a lightly floured surface, then cut into 2.5cm/2in pieces to form the gnocchi. Using the prongs of a fork, make an indentation in the top of each one.

5 For the pesto, grind the sage leaves, pumpkin seeds and salt together in a mortar and pestle, or food processor, to form a paste. Stir in the grated Parmesan and olive oil.

6 Dry fry the pancetta in a frying pan and when the oil starts to be released, stir in the kale and fry until crispy.

7 Push the pancetta and kale to one side of the pan, then fry the sage leaves until crispy. Tip everything on to kitchen paper to drain, and keep warm.

8 Drop the gnocchi into a large pan of boiling salted water and cook for a couple of minutes. They are ready when they rise to the surface of the water. Drain.

9 Plate up the crispy kale and bacon, then either gently toss the gnocchi in the pesto to coat and spoon it on top, or put the nude gnocchi on the plate and drizzle over the pesto.

10 Serve, topped with an anchovy fillet or two, a couple of fried sage leaves, and some extra Parmesan grated over the top.

PASTRAMI

Making your own pastrami is a fairly time-consuming process. However, once you have tasted your own home-made version, a New Yorker-style sandwich from a store will never quite hit the spot again, unless you are actually in New York, obviously. I don't want to get involved in American culinary politics and dictate how to structure such an iconic sarnie, but my preferred way of serving it is influenced by time spent living in Germany, and a love of pickled cabbage and gherkins. You may like it another way. The secret to this rustic pastrami – which is sweet and spicy, smoky and succulent – is the smoked paprika and the slow, hot smoking.

makes: about 1.5–1.8kg/3⅓–4lb
difficulty: 🔥🔥🔥
wood: oak or applewood
equipment: brining tub, kitchen paper, hot smoker, foil, meat probe, conventional oven, rack, baking tray, fork, knife
brining time: 12–15 days
smoking time: 5–6 hours
target temperature: 120°C/248°F

2.5kg/5½lb flat-shaped piece of beef brisket
45ml/3 tbsp black peppercorns
30ml/2 tbsp coriander seeds
2 garlic cloves
5ml/1 tsp chilli flakes
15ml/1 tbsp smoked paprika
bagels, mustard, sliced Monteray cheese, pickled red cabbage, and gherkins, to serve

For the strong brine:

5 litres/8¾ pints water
1kg/2¼lb salt
250g/9oz/1¼ cups sugar

For the sweet brine:

5 litres/8¾ pints water
500g/1¼lb salt
500g/1¼lb sugar

1 Combine the ingredients for the strong brine in a brining tub, add the beef brisket, then cover, chill and leave to cure for 7–10 days.

2 Pour away the strong brine and replace it with the sweet one. Leave to cure for 5 days. Remove the brisket from the brine, and pat it dry with kitchen paper.

3 Set a fire in a hot smoker, preheat it to the target temperature, and prime it with some oak or applewood chips.

4 Prepare the distinctive flavours for the pastrami by crushing the black peppercorns, coriander seeds and garlic. I like it nice and crunchy so use a pestle and mortar and keep it coarse.

5 Vigorously massage the crushed spices, chilli flakes and paprika into the surface of the brisket, trying to get as much to stick to the meat as possible.

6 Put the brisket on a piece of foil to reduce contact with direct heat, yet still allow smoke to circulate, and place a pan of water in the smoker to keep the it moist.

7 Hot smoke the brisket for 3–4 hours, until it has an internal temperature of 90°C/194°F. If it is too hot to comfortably touch then you know you are on track, or if you want to be extra careful, use a meat probe. Try to keep the temperature of the smoker low and steady so the cooking takes as long as possible, and keep chucking handfuls of sawdust or wood chips on the fire to keep it smoky.

8 Preheat the conventional oven to 120°C/25°F/Gas ½. Put the smoked brisket on a rack over a baking tray with 2.5–5cm/1–2in of boiling water in the bottom. Build a foil 'hat' around the meat and seal it up by pinching together the sides of the foil. Aim to create as much free space around the meat as possible to allow the steam to circulate.

9 Cook in the oven for about 2 hours, until it is so tender that a fork can slide into it like a hot knife through butter. Alternatively, you can keep the unwrapped meat in the smoker, but I like really steaming it in a conventional oven for the last cooking stage.

10 Slice the pastrami thinly across the grain while still hot and serve warm in mammoth slices sandwiched in a bagel. It is a sin to serve this without mustard and gherkins, and you can also add thinly sliced cheese and pickled cabbage.

TENNESSEE BARBECUE BRISKET

serves: 12
difficulty: 🔥🔥🔥
wood: hickory
equipment: coffee grinder or pestle and mortar, cold smoker, 2 trays, bowl, brush, foil
curing time: 1 hour
smoking time: >8–12 hours
target temperature: 120°C/250°F

This is the iconic low-and-slow smoked recipe that lies at the heart of a Deep South barbecue. The longer you can set aside to smoke your brisket, the deeper the smoke ring, the better the bark and the more succulent the texture. The flavour is all in the rub and this recipe uses a Tennessee-style combination of spices and herbs that complements a lightly smoked beef. Instead of spreading on a sticky glaze, I mop on a tasty beer marinade every hour or so to keep it moist. Maintain a good, even temperature by adding more lit charcoal if necessary.

4kg/9lb beef brisket
slaw and pickles, to serve

For the rub:

30ml/2 tbsp black peppercorns
15ml/1 tbsp cumin seeds
10ml/2 tsp brown sugar
30ml/2 tbsp sea salt
30ml/2 tbsp paprika
30ml/2 tbsp mustard powder
30ml/2 tbsp ground coffee
15ml/1 tbsp chilli powder
15ml/1 tbsp ground white pepper
1 garlic clove, crushed

For the Tennessee mop:

150ml/^{1}/$_4$ pint/^{2}/$_3$ cup American beer or a
    hoppy light ale like IPA
50ml/2fl oz/^{1}/$_4$ cup cider vinegar
30ml/2 tbsp brown sugar
15ml/1 tbsp garlic purée
15ml/1 tbsp cracked black peppercorns
15ml/1 tbsp chilli flakes
15ml/1 tbsp paprika
5ml/1 tsp of salt

For the slaw:

^{1}/$_2$ red cabbage, finely sliced
4 carrots, grated
2 red onions, finely sliced
2 fennel bulbs, grated
60ml/4 tbsp of mayonnaise
30ml/2 tbsp grated orange zest
juice of 1 orange
15ml/1 tbsp each fresh dill and coriander

1   Blitz all the ingredients for the rub in a coffee grinder or crush with a pestle and mortar. Rub the mixture all over the brisket and leave to cure for 1 hour.
2   Meanwhile, prepare a cold smoker and prime it with hickory chips. Place a tray of water on one side of the grill.
3   Position the brisket fat side up over another tray, away from the hot coals, and smoke for 10–12 hours, checking the temperature regularly. You are aiming for a temperature inside the meat of 90°C/194°F and around 120°C/248°F in the smoker. Add more lit charcoal if you need to and extra hickory chips for a steady light smoke.
4   Mix the Tennessee mop ingredients together in a bowl and after an hour of smoking start basting the brisket with the mop. Repeat every 45 minutes or so.
5   After 8 hours, you can try out a little pitmaster's secret, which is to wrap the cooked brisket in foil for the last hour of smoking.
6   Combine all the slaw ingredients in a large bowl, stirring to coat everything in the mayo.
7   Once the meat is done, thickly slice the meat and serve it with slaw and pickles.

CHORIZO

The word salami comes from the Italian *sale*, meaning salt. Popular myth has it that Roman legionaries were often paid with salt, hence the word salary, but this is only speculation and there is no evidence to back it up. I have to say, though, that I wouldn't mind getting paid in salt as the ability it gives you to cure or season food is phenomenal. I always use at least 2 per cent weight of salt in my chorizo, the Spanish version of salami, preserved sausage flavoured with smoked paprika, and it must be mixed in well – it's important that the salt penetrates all of the pork since this is where a salami or chorizo either succeeds or fails. I use fine table salt for this type of recipe because it is cheap and will get right into the minced pork.

makes: 6
difficulty: 🔥🔥🔥🔥
equipment: knife, sausage mincer (optional), soaked natural sausage casings, sausage machine, butcher's twine, muslin (optional)
air-drying time: 4–6 weeks

2kg/4¹/₂lb pork shoulder
500g/1¹/₄lb pork fat, cured if possible
100g/3³/₄oz/generous ¹/₂ cup salt
8 garlic cloves, finely chopped
30ml/2 tbsp fennel seeds
30ml/2 tbsp smoked paprika
100ml/3¹/₂fl oz/scant ¹/₂ cup red wine
cheese and pickles, to serve

1 If you have a meat mincer, start by chopping your pork shoulder and fat into 2.5cm/1in cubes, then squeeze it through the mincer. Alternatively, buy 2.5kg/5¹/₂lb good-quality minced (ground) pork from your local butcher.
2 Add the salt, garlic, fennel and paprika. Stir well, then add the red wine.
3 Prepare a sausage machine with damp natural sausage casings. Slowly start extruding the sausage mixture into the casings, taking care not to overfill them and trying to keep them an even size.
4 Form the meat into a large ring, then twist it into 20–30cm/8–12in sections, tie off using butcher's twine, and cut it into individual chorizo loops.
5 Hang the loops in a well-ventilated undercover area and leave for 4–6 weeks to air dry. If any white mould forms on the chorizos, clean it off with a vinegar-and-water solution and a piece of muslin. During the hanging process the chorizo ferments, and because of this it has many natural health benefits. For example, it contains lactic acid bacteria that can help maintain a healthy digestive system.
6 Enjoy in slices with a glass of red wine or served on a board with some cheese and pickles for a home-made picnic.

TRY THIS

• German-style sausage – Swap the fennel seeds and smoked paprika for juniper berries and lots of ground black pepper. This is perfect for a rustic lunch served with bread and a pint of beer.
• Pepperoni – Hot-smoked paprika and dried chilli flakes bring heat to this Italian-American favourite. It is a dry sausage that originated from southern Italy and is often made with a blend of cured pork and beef.
• Garlic saucisson – Adding huge amounts of garlic into the mix results in an intense salami that can stand out among an array of other flavours in stews, stuffing or mixed platters.

FRANKFURTERS

makes: 12
difficulty: 🔥🔥🔥
wood: mesquite
equipment: sausage mincer or food processor, soaked natural sausage casings, sausage machine, large pan, kitchen paper, cold smoker
cooking time: 20 minutes
smoking time: 2–3 hours
target temperature: 30°C/86°F

1kg/2¼lb lean pork shoulder
750g/1lb 11oz lean beef
250g/9oz pork belly fat
½ onion, roughly chopped
1 garlic clove
50ml/2fl oz/¼ cup milk
5ml/1 tsp ground coriander
5ml/1 tsp ground mustard
5ml/1 tsp ground white pepper
5ml/1 tsp salt
5ml/1 tsp paprika
2.5ml/½ tsp ground mace
2.5ml/½ tsp dried marjoram

I spent some of my childhood in Germany and my food memories are of Bratwurst, Bavarian smoked sausage and all sorts of other regional sausage specialities. This recipe is my take on that classic hot dog sausage, the frankfurter. The key to a good one is to start out with finely minced meat, season it with plenty of flavourings, parboil it and then cold smoke it low and slow. The resulting frankfurter can then be steamed or grilled and served in a roll with ketchup and/or mustard.

1 Purée the onion, garlic and milk in a food processor until smooth.
2 If you have a sausage mincer, start by chopping the pork, beef and pork fat into 2.5cm/1in cubes, then squeeze these through your mincer using a fine blade. Alternatively, ask your butcher to finely grind the meats for you.
3 Combine the meat with all the remaining ingredients and grind a second time if possible, or mix very well with your hands. Alternatively, a brief blitz in a food processor will help combine the sausage mix and ensure it's a fine texture. Chill for 30 minutes.
4 Meanwhile, prepare your sausage machine with damp natural sausage casings.
5 Slowly start extruding the sausage mixture into the casings, taking care not to overfill them and trying to keep them an even size. Form the meat into a large ring and then twist into 15cm/6in-long links.
6 Parboil the still-joined links in a pan of simmering water for 20 minutes.
7 Remove and put the frankfurters in a bowl of iced water to stop them cooking. Once cold, pat dry with kitchen paper and chill. You can keep them refrigerated for up to 1 week.
8 When you are ready to eat, prepare a cold smoker (see pages 32–33) and prime it with mesquite chips.
9 Add as many frankfurters as you need and leave to smoke for 2–3 hours.

difficulty: 🔥
equipment: grill (broiler) or steamer, knife
cooking time: 10 minutes

frankfurters
good quality brioche hot dog rolls
mustard
ketchup

CLASSIC FRANKFURTERS IN BUNS

1 Reheat as many frankfurters as you need on hot coals, under a grill (broiler) or by steaming them, for about 10–12 minutes, until hot all the way through.
2 Split the rolls in half, add a frankfurter into each and top with accompaniments of your choice.

SMOKED CHIPOLATAS

serves: 6
difficulty: 🔥
wood: applewood
equipment: hot smoker, brush, tongs
smoking time: 25 minutes
target temperature: 180°C/350°F

6 high quality butcher's beef chipolatas
15ml/1 tbsp oil

Smoking a chipolata or other sausage adds real depth of flavour and gives you a great ingredient that you can use to build your own hot dog creation. This recipe is inspired by a Philly cheese steak sandwich, so I've used a classic beef sausage from my local butcher, and then added all the trimmings you'd hope to find at an authentic Philadelphia diner or bar. You could take a similar idea and smoke a spicy chorizo sausage to create your own taco dog, or go for a Tennessee barbecue sauce slathered on smoked brisket for something with a flavour of the Deep South. The world is your dog...

1 Set a fire in a hot smoker, preheat it to the target temperature, and prime it with some applewood chips.
2 Brush the sausages with a little oil and place them in the hot smoker.
3 Hot smoke for 20 minutes, turning them at least once for even smoking.

serves: 6
difficulty: 🔥🔥
equipment: tongs, frying pan, knife
cooking time: about 15 minutes

6 smoked chipolatas
200g/7oz flank beef steak
5ml/1 tsp vegetable oil
115g/4oz green and red bell pepper strips
1 white onion, finely sliced
6 brioche hot dog rolls
115g/4oz/½ cup cheese sauce, warm
salt and ground black pepper, to taste
mustard and/or tomato ketchup, to serve
fresh coriander (cilantro) and sliced spring onions (scallions), to garnish

PHILLY CHEESEDOG

1 While the sausages are smoking, season the steak and then pan fry it in a little oil to your preference. Remove from the heat and leave to rest, covered.
2 Add the peppers and onion to the same pan and cook for about 10 minutes, until softened.
3 Slice the steak very thinly, then start building your cheesedog. Split the brioche rolls, then add a smoked sausage, a few slices of steak, and a spoonful of the peppers and onions.
4 Drizzle over a little cheese sauce, add mustard and/or ketchup, and garnish with fresh coriander and sliced spring onion. Open wide...

SMOKED SPICED SAUSAGES

makes: 8
difficulty: 🔥
wood: mesquite or hickory
equipment: hot smoker, large ovenproof pan, spoon
smoking time: 30–35 minutes
target temperature: 180°C/350°F

8 spiced butcher's sausages

Smoking a spicy sausage can add a whole extra dimension to an already tasty banger, and I like to use them to make Jimmy's Jumbo Gumbo – a dish that I've been serving at barbecue pop-up restaurants for years. It is my ultimate smokehouse comfort food, with the smoked spicy sausage really working well with the black pepper and cajun spice blend to create a dish that's best shared with family and friends straight out of the pot.

1   Set a fire in a hot smoker, preheat it to the target temperature, and prime it with some mesquite or hickory chips. Once there is plenty of dense smoke, add the sausages and smoke them for 30–35 minutes.

CAJUN SMOKED SAUSAGE GUMBO

serves: 4
difficulty: 🔥🔥
cooking time: 50 minutes

60ml/4 tbsp rapeseed oil
2–4 garlic cloves, finely chopped
115g/4oz chopped red bell pepper
115g/4oz chopped celery
115g/4oz chopped onion
8 smoked spiced sausages, sliced
15ml/1 tbsp cracked black pepper
15ml/1 tbsp smoked paprika
5ml/1 tsp each of cumin seeds, fennel
    seeds and dried thyme
1/2 fresh red chilli, seeded and finely
    diced
30–60ml/2–4 tbsp plain (all-purpose)
    flour
150g/5oz/3/4 cup risotto rice
1 litre/1 3/4 pints/4 cups chicken stock
115g/4oz canned or fresh tomatoes,
    chopped
275g/10oz squid
15ml/1 tbsp chopped fresh coriander
    (cilantro), plus extra to garnish
sea salt, to taste
cornbread, to serve

1   Put the oil, garlic, pepper, celery and onion in a large pan and cook for about 10 minutes, until beginning to soften.
2   Add the sliced smoked sausage and all the spices, thyme and chilli to the pan. Cook for 5–10 minutes, stiring, until the sausage starts to brown, then sprinkle the flour into the juices and stir in.
3   Quickly add the rice to the pan followed closely by all the stock and the tomatoes. Cook, uncovered, for 30 minutes at a low simmer, then stir in the squid and fresh coriander and simmer for another 3–5 minutes.
4   Season to taste with salt and serve garnished with more coriander, along with some cornbread, if you like.

BURNT ENDS

serves: 8–10
difficulty: ♨ ♨ ♨
wood: hickory
equipment: hot smoker, food processor or pestle and mortar, heavy ovenproof pan, large bowl
marinating time: 15 minutes
smoking time: 3¼ hours
target temperature: 275°F/140°C

1.6kg/3½lb pork belly, cut into chunks
120ml/4fl oz/½ cup apple juice
115g/4oz apricot jam
50g/2oz clear honey
fries, to serve

For the barbecue spice rub:

30ml/2 tbsp paprika
15ml/1 tbsp soft light brown sugar
15ml/1 tbsp salt
5ml/1 tsp cayenne pepper
10ml/2 tsp garlic powder
5ml/1 tsp coriander seeds
5ml/1 tsp cracked black pepper
2.5ml/½ tsp ground white pepper

Burnt ends are traditionally made from the fatty point end of a slow-smoked brisket that is then cooked again until it's really burned and has a decent bark on it. They are commonly served with beans or in a hot sandwich, but I like this version, made with pork belly instead of beef, with fries.

1   Set a fire in a hot smoker, preheat it to the target temperature, and prime it with some hickory chips.
2   Put all the barbecue spice rub ingredients in a food processor or pestle and mortar and blitz or pound to a fairly fine powder.
3   Coat all sides of the cured belly pork in the rub (you should have some left over) and leave to marinate for 15 minutes.
4   Place the belly cubes fat side down in a heavy ovenproof pan and place in the smoker for 3 hours, drizzling with apple juice every 45 minutes to keep the burnt ends moist.
5   When the meat is tender and easily pulls apart, transfer it to a large bowl and toss the cubes with apricot jam and honey, until evenly coated
6   Return the burnt ends to the pan and cook for anther 15 minutes, until the liquid reduces and the meat is caramelised and has a good outer bark.
7   Serve with hot, crispy fries.

MEXICAN CHICKEN

serves: 2-4
difficulty: 🔥🔥🔥
wood: cherry
equipment: bowl, tray, cold smoker, kitchen paper, meat probe
curing time: 6-8 hours
smoking time: 2 hours
target temperature: 140°C/284°F

75g/3oz/6 tbsp salt
40g/1¹/₂oz/3 tbsp sugar
¹/₂ large chicken, split down the backbone

For the Mexican spice rub:

15ml/1 tbsp paprika
10ml/2 tsp soft light brown sugar
5ml/1 tsp ground cumin
5ml/1 tsp ground coriander
5ml/1 tsp cracked black pepper
5ml/1 tsp dried oregano
5ml/1 tsp garlic powder
2.5ml/¹/₂ tsp cayenne pepper

There will always be a huge difference between pulled pork and chicken, but this recipe isn't about comparing the two, instead it celebrates a cooking method that keeps poultry moist and is perfect in a burger, burrito or taco. Pulled chicken requires relatively low and slow cooking, so as usual, using a cure will give you the best result. The sweet and smoky meat is far less fatty than pork, which makes it a real gateway into Deep South-style barbecue, and I've found it to be especially popular with kids, who love chicken and will try new things, but for whom a pork shoulder or brisket can seem a bit daunting.

1 Combine all the ingredients for the Mexican spice rub in a bowl, then mix 30ml/2 tbsp of it together with the salt and sugar.
2 Rub the mixture all over the chicken, massaging it into the cavity and under the skin where possible, so the flavour can really get into the meat.
3 Leave on a tray in the fridge to cure for 6-8 hours.
4 Preheat a cold smoker (see pages 32-33) and prime it with some cherry wood chips.
5 Rinse off the cure from the chicken under cold water, then pat dry the bird with kitchen paper.
6 Smoke the chicken for 2 hours, turning occasionally, until cooked – use a probe to ensure it has reached at least 74°C/165°F.

PULLED SMOKED CHICKEN TACOS

1 Remove the skin from the smoked chicken and pull the meat apart with your hands or a couple of forks.
2 Make a barbecue sauce by melting the butter in a small pan, then stirring in the Mexican spice rub. Stir over a low heat, then add the lime juice, ketchup, brown sugar and chipotle sauce. Season to taste.
3 Stir the sauce into the pulled chicken. Serve in tacos with pink pickled onions and burnt corn, garnished with fresh coriander.

serves: 4
difficulty: 🔥🔥🔥
equipment: forks, small pan
cooking time: 5 minutes

450g/1lb pulled smoked chicken
50g/2oz/¹/₄ cup butter
15ml/1 tbsp Mexican spice rub (see above)
juice of 2 limes
30ml/2 tbsp tomato ketchup
10ml/2 tsp soft light brown sugar
5ml/1 tsp chipotle sauce
salt, to taste
8 tortillas
pink pickled onions, burnt corn (see Try this), to serve
fresh coriander (cilantro), to garnish

TRY THIS

• The easiest way to make burnt corn is simply to roast some peeled corn on the cob on a barbecue or over a fire, but if you don't have one on the go then you can just char them under a very hot grill (broiler) instead. It's worth brushing them with a little oil or butter first, since this helps prevent them from drying out too much.
• To make pink pickled onions, simply peel a red onion and very thinly slice it into rounds or half-moon shapes (depending on its size). Put these in a dish with a pinch of salt, 5ml/1 tsp caster (superfine) sugar and a splash of white wine vinegar Leave to pickle for 30 minutes or so.

HAY-BAKED CHICKEN

serves: 2
difficulty: 🔥🔥🔥
smoking material: hay
equipment: conventional oven, deep roasting tray, blowtorch, lid or foil, meat probe
smoking time: 25–30 minutes

2 chicken thighs
handful of hay
    pinch of sea salt
pinch of cracked black pepper
30ml/2 tbsp finely chopped chives

Baking in hay is one of the easiest ways to smoke food and is great for small amounts of meat or fish. All you need is a standard oven, a roasting tray and some foil. The dried grass imparts a delicate smoke flavour that works particularly well with chicken. The earthy smokiness is perfect served in tacos together with aromatic wild garlic, and peas and samphire for fresh flavours and a splash of colour.

1 Preheat the oven to 180°C/350°C/Gas 4.
2 Put some of the hay in the bottom of a deep roasting tray, place the chicken on top, then sprinkle over the salt, pepper and chopped chives. Put more hay on top so the chicken is surrounded.
3 Using a blowtorch, light the hay in several places until it is smouldering, then quickly cover the tray tightly with a lid or some foil.
4 Bake for 25–30 minutes, or until the internal temperature of the chicken reaches at least 74°C/165°F. Remove the skin before serving.

HAY-BAKED CHICKEN TACOS WITH WILD GARLIC PESTO

serves: 2
difficulty: 🔥🔥
equipment: food processor or mortar and pestle, frying pan, kitchen paper

hay-baked chicken, skin removed, flesh
    pulled into chunks
10ml/2 tsp olive oil
pinch of salt
4 baby courgettes (zucchini)
4 large, mild fresh chillies
75g/3oz samphire
50g/2oz/½ cup garden peas
juice of ½ lemon
2 flour tortillas
handful of pea shoots
pickled red onion rings (see page 76)

For the wild garlic pesto:

60-90ml/4-6 tbsp chopped wild garlic
    leaves
15ml/1 tbsp olive oil
15ml/1 tbsp grated Parmesan
juice of ½ lemon
pinch of sea salt

1 Put all the ingredients for the pesto in a food processor or mortar and process or pound until smooth. Set aside.
2 Drizzle the chicken skin with oil and a pinch of salt, then fry it in a frying pan until crispy. Set aside on kitchen paper to drain.
3 Add the courgettes, chillies and samphire to the pan and fry for 4 minutes in the chicken fat. Add the garden peas and cook for 1 minute more. Squeeze over some lemon juice to deglaze the pan.
5 Serve the chunks of chicken on warm flour tortillas, with the lemon-dressed vegetables, a few sprigs of pea shoots, some pickled red onion rings and a drizzle of wild garlic pesto. Top with a few strips of crispy chicken skin.

TRY THIS
Wild garlic is available to forage between February and April in the UK. Substitute with fresh mint and pea shoots or rocket when it isn't available.

CHARCOAL SALT-BAKED CHICKEN

serves: 6
difficulty: 🔥🔥
wood: charcoal
equipment: hot smoker, baking sheet, baking parchment, large bowl or pestle and mortar, kitchen shears, skillet, pastry brush
cooking time: 1 hour 20 minutes
target temperature: 180°C/350°F

1 whole chicken
4 pak choi (bok choy)
30ml/2 tbsp butter
30ml/2 tbsp soy sauce

For the salt crust:

1.5kg/3lb 7oz sea salt crystals or rock salt
115g/4oz ash from cherry or apple embers
50ml/2fl oz water
30ml/2 tbsp rice wine vinegar
15ml/1 tbsp ground ginger
5ml/1 tsp ground Sichuan pepper
5ml/1 tsp Chinese five-spice powder
6 egg whites, beaten

Cooking a chicken or fish over embers in a salt crust protects the ingredients from the extreme heat of a barbecue, keeps the flesh moist and, despite the huge quantity of salt, perfectly seasoned. Breaking the salt crust at the table creates a feasting vibe. This take on the technique, which incorporates some smoky wood ash, is inspired by an old Chinese recipe.

1 Set a fire in a hot smoker, preheat it to the target temperature, and line a roasting tray with parchment.

2 Make the salt crust. In a large bowl or with a pestle and mortar, combine the salt, ash and water and stir until you have wet sand-like mixture. Incorporate the vinegar, spices and egg whites. Set aside.

3 Using a sharp pair of kitchen shears, cut the backbone out of the chicken. This is called spatchcocking and allows the chicken to cook more evenly.

4 Spread 1–2 handfuls of the salt crust on the baking parchment, then place the chicken on top, laying it flat. Pile the rest of the salt crust on top. Pat it down like you're building a sandcastle, making sure the chicken is completely covered, so there are no holes or spots of skin peeking through.

5 Bake in the hot smoker for 1 hour and 20 minutes.

6 Put the pak choi and butter in a skillet and add to the oven for the final 20–30 minutes, spooning the butter over the pak choi from time to time. Once it is wilted and golden, dress with some of the soy sauce.

7 Remove the chicken from the smoker, and using a knife or mallet, break open the crust the salt has formed over the chicken. Carefully pick off and discard the crust. Use a pastry brush to remove any loose salt.

8 Peel off and discard the skin (it will be too salty to eat) to reveal the juicy, tender and perfectly seasoned meat underneath.

9 Sprinkle over the remaining soy sauce and serve immediately with the pak choi.

JERK SMOKED BEER CAN CHICKEN

serves: 4
difficulty: 🔥🔥🔥
wood: hickory
equipment: spice grinder or pestle and mortar, hot smoker, heatproof container, pan, meat probe
smoking time: 1½ hours
target temperature: 180°C/350°F

1.8kg/4lb chicken
can of beer
4 sweet potatoes

For the jerk rub:

1 Scotch bonnet chilli, seeded and
　finely chopped
75g/3oz spring onions (scallions),
　finely chopped
30ml/2 tbsp demerara (raw) sugar
15ml/1 tbsp garlic purée
5ml/1 tsp ginger purée
5ml/1 tsp salt
5ml/1 tsp ground allspice
5ml/1 tsp ground ginger
5ml/1 tsp dried thyme
2.5ml/½ tsp grated nutmeg
2.5ml/½ tsp ground cinnamon

For the glaze:

15ml/1 tbsp jerk rub
50ml/2fl oz/¼ cup pineapple juice
50ml/2fl oz/¼ cup ginger beer
60ml/4 tbsp clear honey

For the pineapple and mango salsa:

flesh of ½ pineapple, finely diced
flesh of ½ mango, finely diced
2 spring onions (scallions), finely
　chopped
juice of 1 lime
½ fresh red chilli, finely chopped
salt, to taste
15ml/1 tbsp fresh coriander (cilantro)

Recently, I spent a lot of time working closely with Levi Roots on a range of Caribbean smokehouse recipes inspired by his restaurant, and this jerk rub is a result of many attempts and numerous versions to capture the taste of his Reggae Reggae sauce as a barbecue rub for home. The principle of using a can of beer is the same as hot smoking with a water pan, except that the beer evaporates directly into the cavity of the bird, helping to moisten and flavour the chicken as it smokes.

1　Combine all the jerk rub ingredients in a spice grinder or pound them with a pestle and mortar. Set aside 15ml/1 tbsp of the rub to use in the glaze, then rub the rest all over the chicken, massaging it in well. If you like, leave it overnight in the fridge to marinate, for a smokier end result.

2　Set a fire in a hot smoker, preheat it to the target temperature, and prime it with some hickory chips.

3　Drink half the beer (if you want to!), then push the top three-quarters of the can inside the cavity of the bird so it sits upright. Put the can and the bird in a roasting tin. Place into the preheated smoker and smoke for 1 hour.

4　Warm the remaining jerk spices in a small pan with the pineapple juice, ginger beer and honey and simmer until it thickens slightly.

5　Cut the sweet potatoes in half, half cutting through in thin slices if you wish, and drizzle with olive oil.

6　Brush the chicken generously with the glaze an hour into the cooking time, and add the sweet potatoes to the smoker. Leave it to smoke for another 30 minutes or so, or until the internal temperature of the chicken reaches at least 74°C/165°F and the juices run clear.

8　Leave the chicken to rest for about 20 minutes. Keep the sweet potatoes in the smoker during this time, to finish cooking.

8　Meanwhile, combine all the ingredients for the pineapple and mango salsa. Pull apart the chicken and serve with the baked sweet potatoes and salsa.

SMOKY CHICKEN WINGS

serves: 6
difficulty: 🔥🔥🔥
wood: applewood
equipment: 2 large bowls, wire rack, tray, hot smoker
marinating time: 12 hours
smoking time: 1¼ hours
target temperature: 180°C/350°F, then 150°C/302°F

1kg/2¼lb large chicken wings, cut into flats and drumettes

For the rub:

5ml/1 tsp paprika
2.5ml/½ tsp garlic powder
2.5ml/½ tsp onion powder
2.5ml/½ tsp dried thyme
2.5ml/½ tsp dried oregano
2.5ml/½ tsp ground coriander
good grinding of ground black pepper
generous pinch cayenne pepper

For the sauce:

50g/2oz/¼ cup butter
45ml/3 tbsp Louisiana-style hot sauce
15ml/1 tbsp Worcestershire sauce

Once you've tried these smoked chicken wings you'll never look back. The sweet applewood smoke softens the hot pepper sauce with a background flavour and the dry rub works well with the barbecue roast. I like to sometimes serve these simply, with just a Cajun dry rub, but the sauce adds an extra finger-licking dimension. Traditionally, they are served with a blue cheese dip and some celery sticks, or they can form part of a barbecue spread.

1 Mix the rub ingredients together in a large bowl, then add the chicken wings and toss to ensure they are evenly coated.
2 Ideally, place the wings in a single layer on a wire rack set over a tray, then leave in the fridge overnight.
3 When you are ready to cook, set a fire in a hot smoker, preheat it to the target temperature, and prime it with some applewood chips.
4 Smoke the wings for 30 minutes, then decrease the temperature to 150°C/302°F and roast for a further 45 minutes.
5 Meanwhile, combine the ingredients for the sauce in a large bowl. Add the cooked wings and turn to coat thoroughly before serving.

OLE' SMOKY CHICKEN BURGER

serves: 4
difficulty: 🔥🔥
wood: pecan
equipment: hot smoker, large bowl, plate, clear film (plastic wrap), tongs
chilling time: 30 minutes
smoking time: 10-15 minutes
target temperature: 200°C/400°F

450g/1lb chicken mince (60:40 breast and thigh)
75g/3oz dried apricots, finely chopped
50g/2oz/1 cup fresh breadcrumbs
5ml/1 tsp cumin seeds
2.5ml/½ tsp ground cinnamon
2 garlic cloves, finely chopped
15ml/1 tbsp finely chopped mint
1 egg, beaten
pinch of salt
15ml/1 tbsp flour, for dusting
15ml/1 tbsp oil, for cooking

Building a burger is both an art and a science. You have to consider where the garnish sits in relation to the bun to avoid soggy bread, add just the right amount of sauce, and cook the patty to perfection. For this recipe I've kept the chicken patties moist by adding apricots to the mince and finishing with a generous dollop of harissa mayo. It's important to smoke the chicken minced in a burger rather than smoking it first to keep the burger moist, and flavour the other ingredients.

1 Set a fire in your hot smoker, preheat it to the target temperature, and prime it with some pecan chips.
2 Combine all the burger ingredients in a large mixing bowl, then form into four patties and dust with a little flour.
3 Put the burgers on a plate, cover with clear film and chill in the fridge for at least 30 minutes.
4 Take the chicken burgers out of the fridge and rub them with a little oil. Place on to the grill of the hot smoker and cook for 10-15 minutes, turning as required.

serves: 4
difficulty: 🔥🔥
equipment: 2 small bowls
cooking time: about 5 minutes

30ml/2 tbsp mayonnaise
5ml/1 tsp harissa
200g/7oz halloumi, sliced
4 focaccia buns, split in half
4 smoked chicken burgers
za'atar, for sprinkling (optional)

For the carrot slaw:

1 carrot, grated or shaved
30ml/2 tbsp cider vinegar
10ml/2 tsp honey
5ml/1 tsp cumin seeds
pinch of salt

CHICKEN BURGER WITH MARRAKESH CARROT SLAW

1 Mix together the mayonnaise and harissa in a small bowl. Set aside.
2 To make the carrot slaw, combine all the ingredients in a separate bowl.
3 Put the halloumi and the focaccia, cut side down, on the griddle of the hot smoker and cook on each side until toasted and bar marked.
4 Spread the mayo on one half of the focaccia buns, place the burgers on top, then add a spoonful of slaw, some slices of halloumi and a sprinkling of za'atar.

TANDOORI CHICKEN

serves: 4
difficulty: 🔥🔥
wood: oak
equipment: frying pan, large bowl, clear film (plastic wrap), hot smoker, wooden skewers
marinating time: 1–2 hours
smoking time: 20 minutes
target temperature: 180°C/350°C

This is my take on a UK national treasure – the humble chicken tikka masala. I love a gentle smoked flavour to work with toasted mild spices, and chicken is excellent for soaking up all the aromas and tastes. Threading the chicken on to skewers means it is super easy to put them on the barbecue or in a hot smoker, and they are especially delicious with smoky grilled broccoli, bhajis and a dollop each of cooling yogurt and sweet and spicy mango salsa.

2 large chicken breasts, cut into chunks

For the tikka marinade:

5ml/1 tsp garam masala
5ml/1 tsp cumin seeds
5ml/1 tsp ground coriander
5ml/1 tsp tikka or tandoori spice blend
75ml/5 tbsp natural (plain) yogurt
15ml/1 tbsp oil
5ml/1 tsp salt

1 Start by toasting all the spices for the tikka marinade in a dry frying pan for 2–3 minutes, to release the flavours.
2 Tip the spices into a large bowl and combine with the yogurt, oil and salt.
3 Add the chicken and turn to coat well in the marinade, then cover and leave to marinate for 1–2 hours.
4 Set a fire in a hot smoker, preheat to the target temperature, and prime it with some oak chips. Soak some wooden skewers for at least 30 minutes.
5 Thread the chicken on to the skewers, then place on to the grill and close the door or lid. Cook for 8–10 minutes on each side, until slightly charred.

TANDOORI CHICKEN AND BROCCOLI NAAN-WICH

serves: 4
difficulty: 🔥🔥
wood: oak
equipment: brush, preheated hot smoker, bowl
cooking time: 30–45 minutes
target temperature: 180°C/350°C

1 small broccoli head
1 batch of tikka marinade (see above)
4 mini naans
2 onion bhajis
75ml/5 tbsp natural (plain) yogurt

For the mango salsa:

flesh of 1 mango, diced
1/2 cucumber, peeled and finely diced
5ml/1 tsp chopped fresh mint
5ml/1 tsp finely sliced fresh red chilli
juice of 1 lime

1 Brush the broccoli with the marinade, then place it in the hot smoker or oven before you add the chicken (see above). Cook the broccoli for 30–45 minutes. It is OK if it burns slightly – you just want to avoid ending up with an uncooked, crunchy middle and a charred outside, which is what happens if you cook it too quickly.
2 Prepare a simple mango salsa by combining the ingredients in a bowl.
3 Shortly before you are ready to serve, heat the naans briefly on the griddle.
4 Build your smoked chicken naan-wich by sliding the chicken off the skewer and roughly chopping it. Break off the tandoori broccoli florets, layer up with crumbled onion bhajis and dress with mango salsa.
5 Serve warm with yogurt on the side.

YAKITORI CHICKEN SKEWERS

serves: 2
difficulty: 🔥🔥
wood: cherry
equipment: hot smoker, wooden skewers, small pan, brush
cooking time: 15 minutes
target temperature: 220°C/428°F

450g/1lb diced chicken breast
8 spring onions (scallions), cut into 5cm/2in lengths
15ml/1 tbsp sesame seeds, to garnish

For the yakitori sauce:

50ml/2fl oz/¼ cup soy sauce
50ml/2fl oz/¼ cup mirin or rice wine vinegar
50ml/2fl oz/¼ cup Japanese whiskey or sake
45ml/3 tbsp soft light brown sugar
4 garlic cloves, crushed
10ml/2 tsp grated fresh root ginger

Yakitori has been hailed as the latest dude food trend and the Japanese street food is taking the barbecue world by storm. I love the combination of cherry wood, with its sweet smoky tone, and the Japanese whiskey that I use in my sauce instead of sake. These skewers can be adapted to all sorts of ingredients, so get creative. Once you start playing with the bold flavours and smoke-grilling, you'll be hooked.

1   Set a fire in a hot smoker, preheat it to the target temperature, and prime it with some cherry wood chips.
2   Soak the wooden skewers in water for 30 minutes.
3   Combine all the yakitori sauce ingredients in a small pan, place over a medium heat and simmer for about 15 minutes, stirring frequently so it doesn't stick and burn, until reduced and thickened. Leave to cool.
4   Thread the chicken pieces and spring onions on to the skewers, then brush with the sauce.
5   Cook the chicken for 20 minutes, basting with more yakitori sauce a few times, until cooked and golden.
6   Sprinkle with sesame seeds to garnish.

SMOKED CHICKEN LIVERS

serves: 4-6
difficulty: 🔥 🔥 🔥
wood: oak
equipment: hot smoker, knife, bowl, skillet or heatproof pan
smoking time: 6-8 minutes
target temperature: 190°C/374°F

400g/1lb chicken livers
115g/4oz shallots, finely chopped
30ml/2 tbsp clear honey
5ml/1 tsp olive oil
15ml/1 tbsp apple brandy
pinch of salt

The strong taste of liver is robust enough to take oak smoke, and the resulting flavour sensation is wonderful on its own or as the starring role in a rustic pâté. I use some apple brandy in my recipe for an autumnal note that means the pâté works really well spread on crisp toast and served with a green apple chutney and a glass of Cornish cider.

1　Set a fire in a hot smoker, preheat it to the target temperature, and prime it with some oak chips.
2　Clean the chicken livers, trimming away any fat, then toss in a bowl with the shallots, honey, oil, brandy and salt.
3　Transfer everything to a skillet or suitable heatproof pan and smoke for 3-4 minutes. Turn over the livers and smoke for another 3-4 minutes, then remove from the smoker.

serves: 4-6
difficulty: 🔥
equipment: food processor, ramekins
chilling time: 1-2 hours

smoked chicken livers
100m/3½fl oz/scant ½ cup double (heavy) cream
15ml/1 tbsp Dijon mustard
sprig of thyme
pinch of ground black pepper
150g/5oz/10 tbsp clarified butter
herbs or nettles, rinsed and patted dry, to garnish
toast and chutney, to serve

CHICKEN LIVER PÂTÉ

1　Put the chicken livers in a food processor with the cream, mustard, thyme and pepper and blitz in short bursts until just smooth.
2　Transfer the mixture to ramekins and cover the surface with clarified butter. I like to place some herbs or a nettle leaf into the butter before it sets, for a garnish.
3　Leave to chill in the fridge for 1-2 hours before eating.
4　Serve with crisp, hot toast or crackers and chutney.

BOURBON-BRINED TURKEY

serves: 12
difficulty: 🔥 🔥 🔥
wood: whiskey oak
equipment: large jug, large plastic container or bag, hot smoker, kitchen paper, bowl, cook's syringe, meat probe, foil, two 4-hole Yorkshire pudding tins (pans) or a 12-hole muffin tin (pan)
brining time: 6–12 hours
cooking time: 5 hours
resting time: 1 hour
target temperature: 200°C/400°F then 180°C/350°F

1 whole turkey
accompaniments, such as steamed
　　vegetables, Yorkshire puddings,
　　bread sauce, cranberry sauce and
　　perhaps some home-made sausages

For the brine:

250ml/8fl oz/1 cup of bourbon
250ml/8fl oz/1 cup water
150ml/¼ pint/⅔ cup maple syrup
75g/3oz/6 tbsp salt
4 cloves
grated zest of 1 orange
1 bay leaf
1 sprig of thyme

For the rub:

5ml/1 tsp paprika
5ml/1 tsp dried thyme
5ml/1 tsp mustard powder
5ml/1 tsp ground coriander
5ml/1 tsp garlic powder
5ml/1 tsp cracked black pepper
5ml/1 tsp sea salt
2.5ml/½ tsp cayenne pepper

Brining poultry in my experience means that it takes on more flavour from a rub or woody tones from a smoker, and it cooks better than if you simply marinate and cook it on the barbecue. This recipe captures a festive feast quality, and is perfect for an informal Sunday lunch or summer family get-together. The bourbon brine is sweetened with maple syrup, and you can add more herbs and spices to suit your tastes. I usually go one stage further and during the roasting, inject the bird with more bourbon to get the flavour deep into the breasts and thigh, which also makes it even more succulent.

1　Prepare the brine by stirring all the ingredients together in a large jug. Place the turkey in a large plastic container or bag and cover with the brine. Leave in the fridge for 6–12 hours. Rotate the turkey every hour or two for an even brining.

2　Set a fire in a hot smoker and leave it to heat up. Strain the turkey, reserving some of the brine solution so you can inject it into the bird to add flavour and moistness during the roasting. Pat the turkey dry with kitchen paper.

3　Combine all the rub ingredients in a bowl and massage all over the turkey.

4　Once the smoker has reached 200°C/400°F, add the turkey and cook for about 40 minutes. At this stage, start injecting the bourbon brine into the thickest parts of the bird every hour or so, and at the same time add some whiskey oak chunks to the smoker.

5　Cook for another 4 hours, allowing the temperature in the smoker to reduce to 180°C/350°F. The turkey is done when the juices run clear and the internal temperature reaches at least 74°C/165°F.

6　Remove the turkey from the smoker, cover with foil and leave to rest for at least 1 hour. Make sure the turkey is on a dish or board that will catch the resting juice – this can be poured into a jug when you are ready to carve, and served alongside the turkey and accompaniments.

7　While the turkey rests, prepare your accompaniments including cooking roast potatoes, roast buttered carrots and Yorkshire puddings, in a preheated conventional oven at 200°C/400°F/Gas 6.

8　Carve the turkey, reheat the juices, and serve with the Yorkshires, potatoes and traditional accompaniments such as bread sauce and cranberry sauce.

FISH

The practice of curing and smoking fish has a rich and varied history that dates back to as early as 1200BC when the Phoenicians were busy trading salted fish across the Eastern Mediterranean. However, it's likely that the basic methods and smoking techniques pre-date this time, with early nomadic peoples commonly cooking fish over wood smoke. This is backed up by the fact that you can find evidence of regional specialities all over the world – from South American citrus-cured ceviche and Portuguese bacalhau or salted cod to gravlax from Scandinavia and a delicious salted fish roe called bottarga in Italy.

Smoked salmon was one of the first trendy British home-grown gourmet foods and has remained popular ever since it first graced our tables. Originally, fresh Scottish salmon was shipped in a little salt to East London where, less than 48 hours after it had been caught, the fish was cured and then transformed into a luxury treat with oak smoke. The process itself hasn't changed much since then, but the trend towards smoked and cured fish has grown in momentum so that there are now artisan smokehouses springing up around the country, and smoked or cured seafood options feature increasingly on restaurant menus. As is often the case, once foods start to appear regularly on menus and we get a taste for them, we want to create them ourselves; this section of the manual will help you to do just that.

CHOOSING YOUR FISH

Generally, fattier fish with more oily flesh, such as mackerel and salmon, are better for smoking, but you can also experiment with smoking shellfish or just curing more delicate white fish. My personal favourites for smoking are salmon, mackerel, trout, eel and smaller fish such as Cornish sardines. The magical alchemy that happens when you combine salt and wood smoke with fish can make your fish feel more meaty and bring out the delicate flavour notes. I also often use sugar for my fish curing as it softens the slightly harsh saltiness and can help encourage the growth of beneficial bacteria such as Lactobacillus.

To help improve the sustainability of the fresh fish you eat, choose to buy at the right time of year. At other times, buy frozen fish, which can be excellent for smoking and curing as unwanted parasites and bacteria should have been killed, providing an extra sense of security for the novice.

FOOD SAFETY

As mentioned on page 50–51, safety is a key consideration when it comes to curing and smoking seafood, and my advice is to always source really fresh, good-quality produce in the first instance. Take a trip to a local fish market early one morning or speak to your fishmonger. Also, carefully follow the instructions on percentages of salt in a cure or smoking times, and maintain good chilled temperatures when storing. Remember, hot-smoked fish isn't dried or preserved in the same way as cold-smoked fish, which means it has a shorter shelf life; smoked fish will keep a week or two or can be frozen for up to a couple of months. Allow it to sit in the fridge for 4–5 hours after it has been smoked, to allow the flavours to mellow and permeate. Wrap it up well in baking parchment and string, otherwise everything else in the fridge will smell of smoke too. Finally, especially with seafood, ensure you clean your work surfaces thoroughly to avoid cross-contamination.

SMOKING WITH TEA

Tea is a great alternative to wood chips for smoking fish, and the oily flesh of mackerel and trout are ideal carriers for the musky smoke. There are many different types of tea out there, but perhaps one of the best is lapsang souchong, which naturally has a lovely smoky aroma.

To tea smoke fish, cure a couple of fillets and then line a large pan with a layer of foil (so that you don't ruin it), and then add a handful of long grain rice, a handful of demerara (raw) sugar and a handful of loose-leaf tea. Add another layer of foil, but make a few small holes in it so the smoke can get through. Lightly oil the skin side of the fish and place it on the foil. Pop the lid on and turn the heat on to medium for a couple of minutes, until smoke starts appearing. Turn the heat to low for 10 minutes, then turn it off altogether and leave the pan to stand for another 10 minutes, so the fish can absorb the smoke. The fish should be perfectly cooked at this point. Make sure you lift the lid off outside if you have a sensitive smoke alarm! The fish can then be enjoyed as it is with a salad, turned into a pâté, or flaked into pasta.

CATCH YOUR OWN

When considering smoking and curing fish at home try to get out fishing first. I'm lucky enough to live near the sea in Cornwall where the fishing is good, but you can find trout in many inland rivers, while mackerel – especially in the warmer months – are running in good numbers around the coast and can be easy to catch simply casting from the shore. You may be fortunate enough to have a friend with a boat who'll take you out for a special fishing day trip, but if not, treat yourself and book on to a boat next time you're on holiday, rand take a portable smoking stove. The level of excitement that comes from catching a fish never fades, but getting to take it home, cure it, smoke it and serve it up is almost unbeatable. There is something immensely satisfying about the simplicity it all.

SMOKED MACKEREL

Kippers are one of my favourite types of whole smoked fish, and they make for a delicious brunch dish served with kedgeree or a poached egg. Traditionally, a kipper was almost always a cured and cold-smoked herring, but I like to kipper mackerel when it's running in Cornwall over the summer and is in plentiful supply. Oily fish works best with this method, which is very simple – the only vaguely tricky step is butterflying your fillets to expose the maximum surface area for smoking, but even that isn't especially hard.

serves: 2
difficulty: 🔥🔥
wood: oak
equipment: knife, kitchen paper, dish, hooks, cold smoker, tray of ice
curing time: 30 minutes
smoking time: 6-8 hours
target temperature: less than 30°C/86°F

2 whole mackerel
75g/3oz/6 tbsp salt
25g/1oz/2 tbsp sugar

1 To butterfly the fish, lay it on its belly and cleanly slice along the backbone, through the head and into the body cavity. Be careful not to cut through the stomach.

2 Remove the guts with some kitchen paper and give the fish a rinse with some cold running water. Pat dry, then press it flat and pop out the eyeballs so that you can easily hang it to smoke later.

3 Place the butterflied mackerel fillets into a dish. Mix together the salt and sugar and sprinkle over the mackerel to cover, then leave for 30 minutes.

4 Rinse, pat dry, then hang up using hooks through the eye holes to air dry while you prepare a cold smoker (see page 32–33). Prime the smoker with tightly packed oak sawdust and allow a dense smoke to form.

5 Hang the whole fish in the smoker, ensuring there's good circulation, and insert a tray of ice to keep the temperature lower than 30°C/86°F. Smoke for 6–8 hours, replenishing the ice tray as needed.

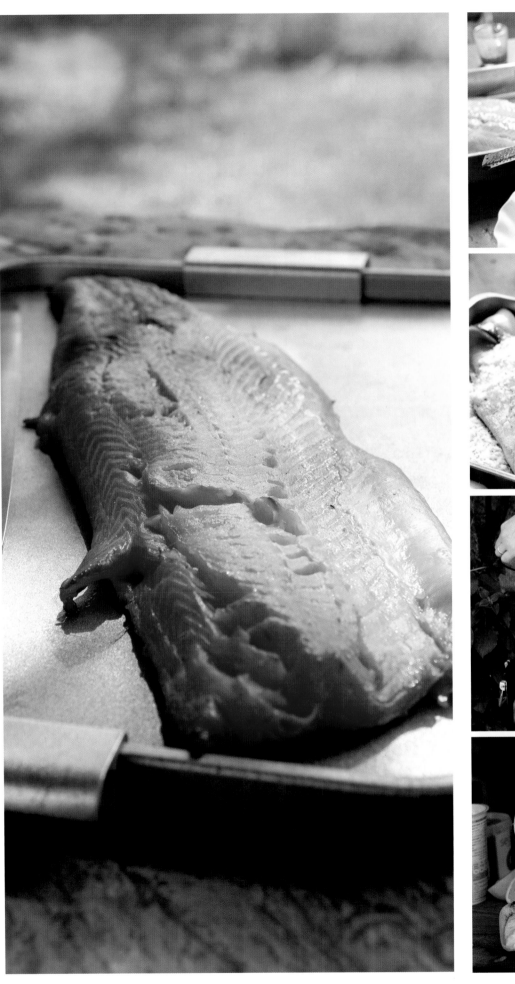

SMOKED SIDE OF SALMON

serves: 6
difficulty: 🔥🔥🔥
wood: applewood and oak
equipment: knife, fish tweezers or needle-nose pliers, bowl, large lidded container, kitchen paper, skewer, 3-4 hooks, wire rack, cold smoker
curing time: 24-48 hours
soaking time: 30 minutes
air-drying time: 2-3 hours
smoking time: 10-12 hours
target temperature: 25°C/77°F

1 side of salmon, skin on

For the cure:
175g/6oz/generous ³/₄ cup salt
40g/1¹/₂oz/3 tbsp soft light brown sugar
15ml/1 tbsp fennel seeds
15ml/1 tbsp yellow mustard seeds
15ml/1 tbsp cumin seeds
15ml/1 tbsp cracked black pepper
grated zest of 1 lemon
2 bay leaves

Smoked salmon is an iconic smoked food that you can have a go at at home and, although the fresh fish is expensive, for a special occasion it is really worth it. If possible, buy wild salmon – its muscle tone is firmer than that of its farmed counterpart. If you can only get a farmed salmon, don't hang it or you'll run the risk of it falling apart. Instead, cut it into fillets before curing, and smoke them flat on a wire rack instead.

1   Trim off the fat flap that runs along the belly of the salmon, as this can turn rancid. Run your fingers over the flesh, feeling for the sharp ends of pin bones. Pull out any you find with fish tweezers or needle-nose pliers.
2   Make the cure by combining all the ingredients in a bowl. Spread one-third of the cure over the bottom of a lidded container large enough to hold the fish. Lay the salmon fillet on top, then spread the remaining cure over so it covers the fish completely.
3   Close or cover the container and store in your fridge for 24-48 hours. A typical side of smoked salmon may lose 16-18 per cent of its weight after curing.
4   Rinse off the cure under cold running water, then soak the salmon in cold water for 30 minutes, to draw out some of the saltiness. Drain well and pat dry.
5   Pierce the salmon with a skewer three or four times, slot in the hooks and suspend it from a wire rack for 2-3 hours, until it feels a bit tacky to touch.
6   Prepare a cold smoker (see page 32-33) and prime it with a combination of applewood and oak chips as a 50:50 mix, ready for a 10-12-hour smoke.
7   Cold smoke the salmon, suspended from the wire rack, until the flesh is bronzed with smoke and feels slightly leathery.
8   Keep covered in the fridge for 12 hours to settle the flavours, and enjoy thinly sliced the next day.

CHARRED CUCUMBER RAITA

makes: 1
difficulty: 🔥
equipment: barbecue or hot smoker
cooking time: 20-30 minutes
target temperature: 220°C/425°F

1 cucumber
15ml/1 tbsp olive oil
salt and ground black pepper, to taste
225g/8oz/1 cup natural (plain) yogurt
8 mint leaves, finely chopped
15ml/1 tsp lemon juice
salt and ground black pepper, to taste

This raita works superbly with a side of salmon The char on the cucumber contrasts nicely with the acidity from the yogurt and mixes up the flavours of a classic mint dip. I like to cook my cucumbers over a hardwood log that has lost some of its heat.

1   Rub the cucumber with a little oil, then season. Place over a smouldering hardwood log or over smoking embers of a barbecue with a few cherry wood chips. Allow to char near direct heat for 20-30 minutes, until the skin is blackened, turning occasionally. Remove from the heat and leave to cool.
2   Remove the black skin from the cucumber with a peeler and then finely slice or grate the flesh. Mix with the remaining ingredients and chill before serving.

CEDAR PLANK SMOKED SALMON WITH TARTARE POTATO SALAD

Plank smoking fish is a lovely way to gain good control when you are cooking over heat. The plank keeps the fish secure but allows you to move it around depending on where the heat is. I like placing my fish on top of a bed of herbs and aromatic veg, but you can simply smoke straight on to the cedar plank. Two important things to remember: soak your plank in water before you use it, and if you are propping it up at an angle (for instance over an open fire), tack the fish into place with some nails before smoking or it will slide off.

serves: 2
difficulty: 🔥🔥🔥
wood: hickory
equipment: brining tub, cedar plank, kitchen paper, hot smoker
curing time: 2 hours
drying time: 30 minutes
smoking time: 20 minutes
target temperature: 180˚C/350˚F

30ml/2 tbsp salt
10ml/2 tsp sugar
500ml/17fl oz/generous 2 cups water
2 salmon fillets, skin on
handful of fresh herbs
6 lemon slices
450g/1lb new potatoes
salt and ground black pepper, to taste
rustic salad, to serve

For the tartare mayo:

30ml/2 tbsp mayonnaise
15ml/1 tbsp finely chopped capers
15ml/1 tbsp finely chopped parsley
15ml/1 tbsp finely chopped dill
15ml/1 tbsp diced gherkins
grated zest of 1 lemon
drizzle of olive oil
pinch of sea salt
pinch of bee pollen (optional)

1 Dissolve the salt and sugar in the water in a brining container and add the fish. Weight the fish down in the cure so it doesn't float. Leave to brine for at least 2 hours in the fridge.

2 Meanwhile, soak the cedar plank in water for 1 hour before use.

3 Remove the lightly cured salmon fillets from the brine and pat it dry with kitchen paper.

4 Set a fire in a hot smoker, preheat it to the target temperature, and prime it with some hickory chips.

5 Arrange the herbs on the plank and place the salmon, skin side down, on top. Season the fish and top with lemon slices. Leave to stand at room temperature for 30 minutes to dry out.

6 Smoke the fish for 20 minutes, until golden and just cooked through.

7 Meanwhile, boil the potatoes in a large pan of lightly water for about 20 minutes or until cooked. Drain, then set aside to cool slightly.

8 Combine all the tartare mayo ingredients in a large bowl, then add the warm potatoes and stir to combine. Transfer the potato salad to a serving bowl and garnish with a little chopped dill and a pinch of bee pollen, if using.

9 Serve the salmon with the potato salad, together with a green salad of baby leaves and herbs on the side.

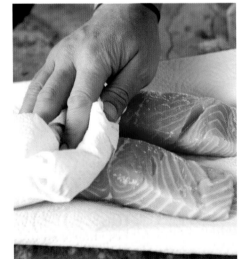

BEETROOT AND WHISKEY-CURED SALMON

serves: 4
difficulty: 🔥🔥
equipment: food processor or pestle and mortar, clear film (plastic wrap), 2 plates, a weight, kitchen paper, knife, small pan, Kilner jar
curing time: 24–36 hours
pickling time: 24 hours
target temperature: <5°C/41°F

1 beetroot, peeled and grated
75ml/5 tbsp whiskey
60ml/4 tbsp salt
30ml/2 tbsp granulated sugar
grated zest of 1 orange
750g/1lb 11oz side of salmon, skinned and deboned

This dish is inspired by the Scandinavian smørrebrød (open sandwich) open sandwiches of cured fish and pickles laid on top of thin slices of rye. I love the contrast of colour you get from the beetroot cure, which not only looks visually impressive but adds real depth of flavour. The alternative would be to make a more classic gravlax with your salmon by simply adding lots of chopped dill in the cure with some black pepper. If you want to really go for a pink colour theme, try my pink pickled eggs.

1 Blitz the beetroot, whiskey, salt and sugar with orange zest in a food processor or with a pestle and mortar, then rub the cure into the salmon.
2 Wrap the salmon tightly in clear film and leave it in the fridge pressed between two plates with a weight on top – evenly placed cans are ideal.
3 Cure for 24–36 hours. The longer you leave it, the stronger the cure.
4 Scrape off the cure carefully and rinse the fish under cold water. Pat dry with kitchen paper and slice thinly.

SALMON SMØRREBRØD WITH PINK EGGS AND CABBAGE

serves: 4
difficulty: 🔥🔥
equipment: small pan, Kilner jar, knife
steeping time: 10 minutes
pickling time: 24 hours

5ml/1 tsp yellow mustard seeds
1 bay leaf
300ml/½ pint/1¼ cups red wine vinegar
115g/4oz/generous ½ cup sugar
200g/7oz sliced red cabbage
6 hard-boiled eggs, peeled
½ cucumber
beetroot and whiskey-cured salmon
6 slices of toasted pumpernickel or rye bread
15ml/1 tbsp chopped dill, to garnish

1 On a medium heat, warm the mustard seeds, bay leaf, vinegar and sugar in a small pan. Bring to a boil, then remove from the heat and add the cabbage. Stir and leave for 10 minutes to steep.
2 Peel the eggs, then layer with the cabbage and pickling liquor in a Kilner jar, seal and leave for at least 24 hours.
3 When you are ready to serve, cut the pink pickled eggs in half or into slices. Peel the cucumber and slice into long, thin strips. Arrange the eggs, cucumber and salmon on top of the bread. Sprinkle with dill to garnish and serve.

EARL GREY AND GIN-SMOKED TROUT WITH HOLLANDAISE

I spent quite few years working for Tregothnan – an old Cornish estate dating back to 1334 that's the home of the original Earl Grey and is now a successful tea plantation. During my time blending teas, I also got to experiment with recipes that incorporate their tea for hot food and cocktails. Smoking is one of the best uses for this lovely ingredient, especially bergamot-scented Earl Grey, and I like to use it to smoke gin-cured trout to build a botanical background to the delicate smoke aroma. Cure your trout before smoking so that the smoke can be absorbed more deeply but also to impart some interesting flavour. This is especially delicious served with a gin and tonic, or a cup of cold-brewed Earl Grey iced tea.

serves: 2–4

difficulty: 🔥🔥

equipment: bowl, hot smoker, kitchen paper, bowl, whisk, frying pan

smoking material: 30ml/2 tbsp Earl Grey tea leaves, 115g/4oz rice, 50g/2oz sugar

curing time: 1–2 hours

smoking time: 10 minutes

target temperature: 110°C/220°F

4 trout fillets, skin on

250g/9oz samphire and/or asparagus, to serve

For the cure:

45ml/3 tbsp caster (superfine) sugar

30ml/2 tbsp salt

50ml/2fl oz/¼ cup gin

15ml/1 tbsp grated lemon zest

4 juniper berries, crushed in a pestle and mortar

For the hollandaise:

4 egg yolks

250g/9oz/generous 1 cup clarified butter, melted

juice of ½ lemon

5ml/1 tsp Dijon mustard

5ml/1 tsp seaweed flakes

1 Combine all the cure ingredients in a bowl. Add the trout fillets and rub the cure all over them. Leave in the fridge for 1–2 hours.

2 Set a fire in a hot smoker, preheat it to the target temperature, and prime it with the tea leaves, rice and sugar mixture.

3 Gently wash the cure off the trout fillets under a running cold tap, pat dry with kitchen paper and place in the hot smoker.

4 Leave to smoke for 5 minutes, until a meat probe inserted into the fish reads 62°C/143°F, then remove from the smoker and set aside to rest. Make a simple hollandaise by beating the egg yolks until smooth, then slowly drizzling in the melted butter, whisking continuously. Add the lemon juice and mustard and stir in carefully.

5 Once the sauce has come together, sprinkle in the seaweed flakes, cover and leave somewhere warm.

6 Cook the samphire and/or asparagus in a frying pan with a little oil.

7 Serve the smoked trout with the samphire and asparagus together with a generous spoonful of seaweed hollandaise.

TRY THIS

Experiment with jasmine, lapsang souchong and other botanical teas for interesting aromas. Chamomile works really well with a delicate fillet of sea bass and manuka tea is also worth trying with mackerel, finished with a sweet honey, sesame and soy glaze. You can also mix wood chips with the tea for a more complex woody note.

SMOKED SARDINES

serves: 4
difficulty: 🔥🔥
smoking material: large handful of chopped lemon peel and 4 sprigs of thyme
equipment: tray, clear film (plastic wrap), cold smoker, kitchen paper
curing time: 30 minutes
smoking time: 20 minutes
target temperature: 50°C/122°F

12 sardine fillets
200g/7oz/1 cup salt
100g/3¾oz/½ cup sugar
15ml/1 tbsp olive oil, plus extra for storing

Sardines are ideal for smoking as they have a high oil content, which means they stay juicy and take on the smoke flavours really well. I then like to marinate the sardines in a spicy, citrussy pickle marinade for my Cornish twist on Catalan escabeche – a dish that's full of fresh flavours and a real taste of summer.

1 Put the sardine fillets in a tray and cover with the salt and sugar. Cover and leave to cure for 30 minutes in the fridge.
2 Prepare and light a cold smoker (see page 32–33) and add some lemon peel and the thyme.
3 Rinse the fish under cold running water and pat dry with kitchen paper.
4 Gently oil the sardines and place on the top shelf of your smoker. Leave to smoke for 20 minutes.
5 Store in a little extra oil in a sealed container if you aren't eating them immediately.

serves: 4
difficulty: 🔥🔥
equipment: frying pan
cooking time: about 10 minutes
marinating time: at least 12 hours

30ml/2 tbsp olive oil
6 garlic cloves, finely sliced
1 red onion, thinly sliced
1 large carrot, sliced
15ml/1 tbsp smoked paprika
5ml/1 tsp picked fresh thyme leaves
5ml/1 tsp finely chopped tarragon
175ml/6fl oz/¾ cup white wine
150ml/1/4 pint/⅔ cup sherry vinegar
1 cinnamon stick
1 bay leaf
15ml/1 tbsp lemon peel strips
15ml/1 tbsp orange peel strips
red bell pepper salsa, to serve

CITRUS-MARINATED SMOKED SARDINES

1 Heat the oil in a frying pan, add the garlic and cook for 2 minutes, until starting to soften. Add the onion and carrot and cook for 3–4 minutes.
2 Season with paprika and the herbs, then pour in the wine and vinegar and add the cinnamon stick, bay leaf and orange and lemon peel strips. Bring to a boil, then remove from the heat and leave to cool to room temperature.
3 Pour the citrus marinade over the smoked sardines and leave in the fridge to marinate for at least 12 hours.
4 Serve in clean sardine tins, or on plates, with some red pepper salsa.

Cornish
Pilchard Fillets
in extra virgin olive oil

SMOKED SHELLFISH

serves: 4
difficulty: 🔥🔥🔥
wood: applewood
equipment: hot smoker
smoking time: 5-7 minutes
target temperature: 220°C/425°F

1kg/2¼lb mussels, debearded,
    thoroughly cleaned and checked
12 oysters, shucked and checked over
12 large king prawns (jumbo shrimp)

Smoked mussels, oysters or cockles have a robust taste of the sea that instantly conjure up a nostalgic beach barbecue experience. I'd recommend serving it with a salsa for a really fresh snack or frying them in batter for a smoky New Orleans-style dish. Alternatively, why not have a go at my signature Cornish seafood dish – it's simple, rustic, full of flavour and heavily inspired by the coast of Cornwall.

1 Set a fire in a hot smoker, preheat it to the target temperature, and prime it with some applewood chips. Place all the shellfish on the grill and close the lid.

2 Smoke for 5-7 minutes, until the shellfish has all cooked and the mussels have opened. Discard any that remain shut.

---

serves: 4
difficulty: 🔥🔥
equipment: hot smoker, skillet
cooking time: 5-7 minutes
target temperature: 220°C/425°F

30ml/2 tbsp oil
3 garlic cloves, finely sliced
1 fennel bulb finely sliced
1 fresh red chilli, thinly sliced
450g/1lb cherry tomatoes or roughly
    chopped heritage tomatoes
smoked shellfish
2 limes
175ml/6fl oz/¾ cup white wine
450g/1lb samphire
30ml/2 tbsp chopped fresh coriander
    (cilantro)
focaccia, to serve

SMOKED SHELLFISH WITH SAMPHIRE AND SUMMER VEG

1 Heat some oil in a skillet, add the garlic and cook for 2-3 minutes, until starting to soften.

2 Add the fennel, chilli, tomatoes and smoked shellfish, then squeeze in the lime juice and pour in the white wine. Deglaze the pan, then mix in the samphire and chopped coriander.

3 Cook for another 1-2 minutes, then remove from the heat and serve with fresh focaccia to mop up the delicious juices.

COOK'S TIP
When checking over shellfish, you are looking for any that smell 'fishy' or whose shells are cracked or open. If they are open, they should snap tightly shut when tapped. Discard any that you are suspicious about.

SMOKED CRAB

serves: 2
difficulty: 🔥🔥
wood: alder
equipment: bowl, clear film (plastic wrap), hot smoker, foil, wire rack
marinating time: 1 hour
smoking time: 10–15 minutes
target temperature: 220°C/425°F

450g/1lb white crab meat
15ml/1 tbsp Cajun seasoning
30ml/2 tbsp lemon juice
5ml/1 tsp Worcestershire sauce
oil, for greasing

It's best to smoke crab after you've boiled and picked out the meat, so you've got more surface area for the smoke to get into, though you can smoke crab claws as long as you crack them well first. The sweet, smoky, unbelievably delicious crab meat can then be used to make this bad-ass surf 'n' turf version of a club sandwich that combines smoked crab, smoked bacon, egg, greens and spicy sriracha mayo. I got the idea from the popular lobster rolls that are all the rage in New England; soft brioche rolls filled with succulent lobster flavoured with a hint of Cajun seasoning. Yum.

1 Put the crab, Cajun seasoning, lemon juice and Worcestershire sauce in a bowl, cover and leave to marinate for 1 hour.
2 Set a fire in a hot smoker, preheat it to the target temperature, and prime it with some alder chips.
3 Place the crab on a sheet of oiled foil on a wire rack at the top of the smoker. Smoke for 10–15 minutes, turning over once, until it is orange/brown in colour.

SMOKED CRAB CLUB SANDWICHES

serves: 2
difficulty: 🔥

4 slices of soft white bread
30ml/2 tbsp mayo, with a few drops of sriracha stirred in
smoked white crab meat
8 rashers (strips) of cooked smoked bacon, preferably home-made
1/2 cucumber, sliced
1 hard-boiled egg, sliced
handful of crunchy lettuce, mizuna or oriental greens
sea salt, to taste
Cajun-spiced fries, to serve (optional)

1 Layer up your sandwich however you prefer it. My preferred order is: sriracha mayo, crab, egg, cucumber, greens, bacon, but it's entirely up to you.
2 For a real treat, serve with some Cajun-spiced fries (just dust some Cajun seasoning over some regular fries).

SEAWEED-SMOKED CLAMBAKE

I did my first New England-style clambake on a beach on the island of Jersey several years ago, and ever since I have been trying to find ways of capturing the flavour and the feeling of seaside feasting in a similar dish. This is the closest I have come, using seaweed to smoke the shellfish and then finishing the corn and potatoes on the grill with lots of seaweed butter.

serves: 4

difficulty: 🔥🔥🔥

equipment: hot smoker, mallet, foil, brush

smoking material: 30ml/2 tbsp seaweed flakes or fresh seaweed, and 30ml/2 tbsp oak chips

smoking time: 5 minutes

cooking time: about 5 minutes

target temperature: 170°C/325°C

450g/1lb mussels

250g/9oz hard-shell clams or razor clams

2 crab claws

2 butterflied lobster tails (optional)

200g/7oz/scant 1 cup butter, melted

handful of samphire or sea greens

4 garlic cloves, finely sliced

1 shallot, finely sliced

2 lemons, halved

450g/1lb waxy new potatoes, par-boiled

2 corn on the cob, sliced and blanched

1/2 fennel bulb, sliced

275ml/10fl oz/1¼ cups pale ale

30ml/2 tbsp fresh coriander (cilantro) and parsley, finely chopped

1 Set a fire in a hot smoker, preheat it to the target temperature, and prime it with some fresh seaweed or seaweed flakes, and oak chips.

2 Prepare the shellfish by debearding the mussels, purging the clams in some running water to remove any grit or sand, and cracking the crab claws with a mallet. It's easiest to ask your fishmonger to butterfly the lobster tails for you, if you're using them.

3 Arrange all the shellfish on a foil-lined tray. Melt 150g/5oz/10 tbsp of the butter and drizzle or brush it over the seafood.

4 Cook for 5 minutes in the smoker, until the shellfish open up and are cooked.

5 Meanwhile, put the remaining 50g/2oz/¼ cup butter, garlic and shallot in a skillet and cook for 2–3 minutes, until softened.

6 Place the lemon halves, cut side down, on the griddle.

7 Add the potatoes, corn and beer to the skillet and cook for a few more minutes, until the veg are done.

8 Serve everything together, with fresh herbs to garnish.

COOK'S TIP

A clambake is also delicious with mackerel stuffed with lemon and herbs or try smoked spicy sausage added into the ingredients for a tasty surf 'n' turf version.

GAME

Having grown up in the countryside, eating game has been a big part of my culinary training, despite the fact that I'm not an experienced hunter; instead, I've relied on the generosity of neighbours and some good bartering skills. That said, nowadays you don't need to own a gun to enjoy cooking game since there are many butchers who will display game in season, and countless wholesalers and specialist game suppliers who can sell you some venison or local wildfowl.

For me, the native breeds that we have available on our doorstep are the ultimate free-range food and their deep gamey flavour combined with the aromatic notes from wood smoke is a match made in heaven. There's something primal and deeply satisfying about the experience of cooking with wild food and the crackle of a wood fire; in fact, I would go so far as to say that it evokes strong instinctive feelings that can transport you back in time.

Before I lose myself in the woods, I want to raise a few points about sourcing game and the importance of seasonality. For a great deal of food, eating seasonally is linked to produce being grown locally and being available for us to buy soon after it has been harvested or killed. Game – while less variable in terms of taste from month to month than, say, local summer strawberries versus imported ones in winter – is only available fresh during the hunting season, which has been designed for sustainable management of stocks and maintaining healthy numbers of animals in the wild. However, you can often source frozen wild game out of season. The table below is a basic guide to the shooting seasons.

I source all my game from an accredited UK game dealer so that the meat is traceable and ethically killed. Rabbit is a good example of why I do this: farmed rabbit is far less tasty than wild, and often suffers from low welfare standards, being mass-produced in factory farms in Europe. That said, despite the relatively recent increase in popularity of wild rabbit it is still quite hard to source. I am lucky enough to have a good friend who shoots on farmers' land and local estates to keep the numbers down, so he always has a good supply of healthy, myxomatosis-free wild rabbits I can use. If you want to get hold of some I recommend ordering it in advance from your local butcher and asking for wild rather than farmed.

The same goes for venison, which is successfully farmed and professionally shot to provide a sustainable source of delicious meat. It is important for me to know that the people who have shot the deer are professionals who cause the animal as little distress as possible. I do also regularly use locally farmed venison for smoking and really enjoy the quality of the meat.

Wild duck can also be delicious but has a relatively short shooting season, so it is rare in most butcher's shops. For this reason, I often revert to free-range locally farmed duck when wild is not in season.

Other types of game birds are farmed fairly intensively and then released for shooting in season. Pheasants in particular are notorious for being domestically reared game birds that are deliberately fattened up to make them easier to shoot, then set free on large estates where they can be picked off. While I find little appeal in this sport, I do enjoy the fact that it means that over winter you can source cheap and very tasty meat for smoking.

GAME SEASON	
Game type	When it's in season
Pheasant	October–1 February
Partridge	1 September–1 February
Wood pigeon	No closed season
Duck	1 September–31 January (inland)
Common snipe	12 August–31 January
Wild rabbit	No closed season
Roe deer	Bucks: 1 April–31 October
Does	1 November–31 March
Fallow deer	Bucks: 1st August – 30 April
Does	1 November–31 March

AIR-DRIED VENISON JERKY

serves: 12
difficulty: 🔥🔥🔥
equipment: knife, pestle and mortar or food processor, dish or tray, clear film (plastic wrap), kitchen paper, hooks, tray, baking parchment or Kilner jar
curing time: 6-8 hours
drying time: 4-8 days
target temperature 10˚C/50˚F

1kg/2¼lb haunch of venison

For the cure:

10ml/2 tsp salt
30ml/2 tbsp soft light brown sugar
15ml/1 tbsp cracked black
    peppercorns
15ml/1 tbsp coriander seeds
5ml/1 tsp chilli flakes
5ml/1 tsp juniper berries, crushed
30ml/2 tbsp cider vinegar

Venison has a lovely savoury flavour that intensifies if you dry the meat into jerky. This is a classic air-dried method but you can also cold smoke it if you like. You can try the same technique with goat, beef, lamb or even rabbit. Once you've mastered the basics you can also marinate the meat strips after curing and before drying to add extra flavour or chilli heat.

1 Using a very sharp knife, slice the meat along the grain into long steaks. I sometimes freeze the meat a little first so that I can slice it very thinly. Trim off any sinew or fat as this doesn't dry as easily.

2 Pound all the dry cure ingredients together in a pestle and mortar or blitz with a food processor, then mix in the vinegar.

3 Massage the cure into the venison strips, covering the meat, then arrange in a dish or tray in layers.

4 Cover and leave in the fridge for 6-8 hours, turning the meat and massaging in the cure every couple of hours.

5 Remove the meat from the cure and shake off the seasoning. Pat dry with kitchen paper and skewer it on to hooks so you can hang it up.

6 Leave it to dry out in a cool (approximately 10˚C/50˚F), dry place with good airflow for 4-8 days. If it is warmer the meat may dry faster.

7 To prolong the life of your jerky so it'll keep for 2-3 weeks, finish the drying in the oven at 50˚C/120˚F with the door slightly open for a further 4 hours. Suspend the strips from the oven rack, with a tray below to catch any final fat that might drip.

8 Store wrapped in baking parchment or in a sterilised Kilner jar. The jerky will keep for 2 weeks. Eat as an appetizer with a glass of cold beer, or pop it into the kids' lunch boxes.

KALE AND VENISON SMOKED SAUSAGE

makes: 12
difficulty: 🔥🔥🔥🔥
wood: applewood
equipment: sausage mincer or food processor, soaked natural sausage casings, sausage machine, skewer, butcher's string, hooks, tray, cold smoker
drying time: 2 days
smoking time: 12 hours
target temperature: 30°C/86°F

450g/1lb pork shoulder, slightly frozen, then diced

450g/1lb pork belly, diced

1kg/2¹/₄lb venison haunch or shoulder, slightly frozen, then diced

200g/7oz kale, finely chopped

30ml/2 tbsp salt

5ml/1 tsp fennel seeds

5ml/1 tsp dried thyme

5ml/1 tsp ground mustard seeds

5ml/1 tsp cracked black pepper

5ml/1 tsp paprika

pinch of cayenne

Kohlwurst is a German smoked sausage that's normally heavily spiced and served with kale. For my version I've used venison for more flavour and put the kale into the actual sausage mix rather than just serving it on the side. For me, these two ingredients work really well together, giving the sausage an earthy, metallic quality. The sausage will lose some of its flavour in the slow-smoking process, so you really can be generous with the amount of spices you use.

1 If you have a sausage mincer, start by chopping the shoulder, belly and venison into 2.5cm/1in cubes, then squeeze these through your mincer using a fine blade. Alternatively, ask your butcher to finely grind the meats for you.

2 Combine the meat with all the remaining ingredients and grind a second time if possible, or mix very well with your hands or a spoon. Alternatively, a brief blitz in a food processor will help combine the sausage mix and ensure it's a fine texture. Chill for 30 minutes.

3 Meanwhile, prepare the sausage machine with damp natural sausage casings.

4 Slowly start extruding the sausage mixture into the casings, taking care not to overfill them and trying to keep them an even size. Form the meat into a large ring and then twist into 30cm/12in-long links.

5 Once formed, poke the sausages in several places with a skewer to allow the smoke to penetrate the casings, then tie them up with some butcher's string into rings.

6 Hang up to dry on hooks for 2 days in the fridge with a tray positioned beneath them to catch drips.

7 Prepare a cold smoker (see page 32–33), priming it with applewood chips. Transfer the sausages to the cold smoker and leave for 12 hours.

8 The sausages can be kept for 1–2 weeks after smoking if you store them in a sealed container. When you are ready to eat them, fry or grill them until brown and sizzling, and cooked through.

TRY THIS

- These smoked venison sausages are delicious served with boiled potatoes and more kale, or in a hotpot.
- If you don't like kale, try substituting it with some finely chopped cooked chestnuts and dried cranberries, or a combination of juniper berries, grated orange zest and rosemary.
- You can also smoke kale at 200°C/392°F for 5 minutes in a stove-top smoker over applewood. It's delicious served with butter and garlic.

CHERRY-SMOKED PHEASANT

serves: 2
difficulty: 🔥🔥🔥
wood: cherry
equipment: hot smoker, bowl, brush, tongs, meat probe, foil, cleaver
smoking time: 1 hour
resting time: 15 minutes
target temperature: 170°C/338°F

1 whole pheasant, cleaned and hung

For basting:

30ml/2 tbsp fish sauce
15ml/1 tbsp palm sugar
1 fresh red chilli, finely diced
5ml/1 tsp Chinese five-spice powder

Game such as pheasant takes on strong smoky tones really well, but in my opinion it's also a meat that is best cooked quickly rather than low and slow. The muscle is very lean, so rather than cold smoking, I hot smoke it, letting some flames lick the skin for a charred finish. I love cherry smoke with pheasant and serve a sharp cherry sauce alongside.

1 Set a fire in a hot smoker, preheat it to the target temperature, and prime it with cherry wood.
2 Mix together the basting ingredients in a bowl, then spread them all over the pheasant.
3 Place the pheasant on the grill and close the smoker.
4 Turn the pheasant after 20 minutes, baste it again, then cook until the flesh is slightly tense or reads at least 74°C/165°F on a meat probe.
5 Remove the pheasant from the smoker, cover it with foil and leave it to rest for at least 15 minutes. Cut into six large chunks and serve.

ASIAN-STYLE SMOKED PHEASANT SALAD WITH CHERRY SAUCE

1 Put all the ingredients for the cherry sauce in a blender and blitz until smooth.
2 Transfer to a pan and heat for 5-10 minutes, until thickened and heated through. You can sieve it to make it smoother, but I prefer some body to a sauce.
3 For the chopped salad, start by frying off some kale in a drizzle of sesame oil until crispy. Drain on kitchen paper, then toss with spring onions, cucumber and carrot and garnish with some sesame seeds if you like.
4 Serve the salad with the pheasant and the sauce on the side for pouring over.

TRY THIS

For a wilder, foraged version of this recipe, using the same methods, try a combination of woodland ingredients for the salad, such as nettles, wood sorrel and purslane. If you want to baste the pheasant during the hot smoking, consider some elderberry syrup and cracked Alexander seeds for seasoning. Serve with a wild garlic pesto (see page 83) on top of the smoked bird.

---

serves: 2
difficulty: 🔥🔥
equipment: blender, pan, sieve (optional), frying pan, kitchen paper
cooking time: 5-10 minutes

cherry-smoked pheasant

For the cherry sauce:

12 cherries, stoned (pitted)
1 star anise
15ml/1 tbsp soy sauce
5ml/1 tsp grated fresh root ginger
15ml/1 tbsp sesame oil
juice of 1 lime
10ml/2 tsp cornflour (cornstarch)
60ml/4 tbsp caster (superfine) sugar

For the chopped salad:

bunch of crispy kale
drizzle of sesame oil
small bunch of spring onions (scallions), sliced into strips
½ cucumber, sliced into strips
1 carrot, sliced into strips

ORANGE-SMOKED DUCK

serves: 2
difficulty: 🔥 🔥 🔥
smoking material: cherry wood and roughly diced peel from 4 oranges
equipment: knife, skewer, curing tub or zip-lock bag, hot smoker, kitchen paper
curing time: 2–4 days
smoking time: 10 minutes
target temperature: 107°C/225°F

2 duck breasts

For the cure:

grated zest of 1 orange
2 star anise
100g/3³/₄oz/generous ¹/₂ cup salt
45ml/3 tbsp soft light brown sugar
bunch of thyme

Duck and orange is a classic combination, but rather than coating duck in a rich orange sauce I like to mix it up by using the ingredients in unexpected ways. Here, smoking the orange peel itself, as well as using the zest in the cure, gives off a fresh citrus smoke that can also work well with fish.

1. Trim off any loose fat from the duck breasts, then push a skewer about halfway into the breast on the skin side several times. I don't trim off the skin as I like to finish the duck in a pan once it's smoked, but you could remove it at this stage and use it make some of your own duck 'quackling' later.
2. Mix together the cure ingredients, then place a layer in the bottom of a container or bag. Rub some more into the duck breasts, completely covering them. Leave to cure in the fridge for 2–4 days.
3. Set a fire in a hot smoker, preheat it to the target temperature, and prime it with cherry wood chips and the orange peel. I use a stove-top smoker for this so that I can keep the meat rare. Wash off the cure off the breasts and pat dry .
5. Smoke the duck breasts for 5 minutes over a high heat, then switch off the heat and leave the duck to rest in the hot smoker for another 5 minutes.

ASIAN-STYLE SMOKED DUCK PANCAKES WITH LAZY KIMCHI

serves: 2–4
difficulty: 🔥 🔥
equipment: knife, large pan
cooking time: about 10 minutes
pickling time: 1–2 weeks
resting time: 5 minutes

2 smoked duck breasts
15ml/1 tbsp soy sauce
5ml/1 tsp clear honey
8 Chinese-style rice pancakes or wraps
salt and ground black pepper, to taste
5ml/1 tsp sriracha sauce

For the lazy kimchi:

12 radishes, finely sliced
¹/₂ small cabbage, shredded
1 carrot, finely sliced
30ml/2 tbsp spring onions (scallions)
275ml/9fl oz/1 cup cider vinegar
75g/3oz/6 tbsp sugar
5ml/1 tsp finely chopped garlic
5ml/1 tsp grated fresh root ginger
5ml/1 tsp gochujang chilli paste

1. To make the lazy kimchi, mix all the sliced vegetables together in a large bowl. Chop the spring onions and add to the bowl.
2. Warm the vinegar and sugar in a large pan until dissolved, then add the garlic, ginger and gochujang chilli and pour over the vegetables. Stir to combine well. Leave to cool, then transfer to an airtight jar and keep in the fridge for 1–2 weeks.
3. When the duck has finished smoking, score the skin with a diamond pattern, season, then place skin side down in a cold frying pan. Turn on the heat to medium-high, so the fat starts to render, and cook for a few minutes on each side, so you get a nice crispy finish.
4. Finish by glazing with the soy sauce and honey. Leave to rest for at least 5 minutes, then carve into thin slices.
6. Open out the pancakes or wraps, then layer on the duck slices and kimchi, drizzle with sriracha and roll up.

TRY THIS
- If you enjoy smoking the duck with orange, then why not try the same method with pink grapefruit or a combination of types of dried peel.
- You could substitute the duck for whole carrots if you wanted a vegan option with a twist. I'd smoke them over manuka and orange peel and then thinly slice and toss them in a soy sauce and honey glaze.

VEGETABLES
FRUIT, NUTS & DAIRY

This is definitely my favourite chapter of this manual because it has given me the chance to experiment with new recipes that I've not tried before. What's more, I've loved flipping the outdated stereotype of smoking and curing being artisan skills reserved for men – grilling on the barbecue while salads are prepared indoors, for example – and feeling free to try something different.

The recipes have all been inspired by what's achievable with basic smoking methods, taking into consideration the taste and texture of each ingredient and working out how best to enhance its natural qualities. That said, smoking vegetables, fruit, nuts, butter and cheese works in much the same way as it does for other foods, and you can apply the same principles to pretty much any ingredient. Adding a coating to the item you want to smoke helps bond the smokiness and enhance the flavour, so smoked nuts, for example, are first brushed with a little oil or butter to allow the smoke to work its way in. Similarly, you can cure fruit or vegetables to help draw out the moisture a little and then hit them with a smoking session. If you are curing wet fruit and vegetables, consider using a salt and sugar blend, or you can throw caution to the wind and simply smoke whole items, such as an aubergine (eggplant) in a hot smoker or a pineapple above an open fire.

VEGETABLES

There has never been a more exciting time to smoke vegetables than right now. Chefs and restaurants are being forced to up their game and become more innovative rather than settling for a token vegetarian option on their menus. Instead of being an afterthought, the vegetable dish can have real wow factor, and smoking is one great way to provide this. Hot smoking whole vegetables is great fun, or, as for meat, you can break down your veg and cold smoke smaller parts. Some vegetables can also be smoked and used in desserts – for example smoked beetroot chocolate brownies, smoked pumpkin pie with maple and pecan, or even a smoked carrot cake with cardamom. My advice would be to practise and plan smoking with fruit and veg so that if you have a vegetarian guest coming for a meal or are just having a meat-free day, your dish is something that you can be truly proud of. Be creative, have fun, and remember that these recipes aren't just side dishes – they can be the main event!

FRUIT

Lots of fruits take on smoky flavours and the woody tones of caramel really well and can be delicious as a dessert after a family barbecue or even in cocktails. There isn't a rule book, so feel free to experiment and invent your own crazy combinations. Try covering blueberries in hay and smoking them for a fire-baked blueberry pie, hot smoking mango on the grill with a chilli and coriander (cilantro) sweet glaze, charring watermelon and serving it with feta salad or, one of my favourites, simply smoking strawberries and serving them with black pepper meringues. My advice for these is to use sweeter wood such as cherry or apple, or for a bacon jam-style aroma try maple and hickory.

CHEESE

When it comes to smoking cheese, the technique is more specific, and it is well worth trying at home as the taste of true smoked cheese is so much better than that of any commercial 'smoked flavour' cheese that has just been dipped in liquid smoke. You can smoke any sort of cheese; once you start having a go, you'll find you're loading your smoker with mozzarella, halloumi, Cheddar and all sorts of other types. I would, however, suggest using a hard cheese to start with and keeping it to around 500g/1¼lb; the last thing you want is to oversmoke an expensive truckle while you're learning the ropes. Once you've got the hang of it, smoking fresher soft cheese is a lovely thing to try. I'd recommend light smoking or even wrapping your cheese in soaked nettle or wild garlic leaves to keep it low and slow.

The key thing to remember is that so long as the temperature of your smoker is less than 35°C/95°F then pretty much anything goes. Any hotter and you are asking for trouble... When I built my first smoker more than 15 years ago, I learned the difference between hot and cold smoking the hard way by putting cheese on a wire grill too close to the sawdust. It was messy to say the least! Needless to say, since then I've designed all my smokers so there's a greater distance between the smoke source and the grill, and I also include water trays and keep a closer eye on the temperature.

TOP TIPS FOR SMOKING CHEESE

- Let your cheese 'chambre' for an hour or two at room temperature before you smoke it. This helps a skin to develop, which protects it.
- For softer cheese, glaze the outside with a little oil, melted butter or syrup before smoking it.
- Smoke cheese in smaller lumps rather than entire truckles, to mitigate the impact on your wallet if it goes wrong.
- If your cheese sweats or oils off in the smoker, whip it out, wrap it in cheesecloth then return it to the smoker.
- Wrap your cheese in foil or clear film (plastic wrap) after smoking it and wait for 2–3 days before eating, to allow the flavours to settle in. Good smoked cheese comes to those who wait...

SMOKED MUSHROOM BURGER

serves: 4
difficulty: 🔥🔥
wood: applewood
equipment: hot smoker, bowl, brush, skillet (optional)
smoking time: 10 minutes
target temperature: 115°C/239°F

30ml/2 tbsp olive oil
2 garlic cloves, finely chopped
4 large portobello mushrooms
115g/4oz blue cheese, crumbled
30ml/2 tbsp butter
4 brioche rolls, smoked tomato ketchup
   and mixed salad, to serve

The trend towards a decent plant-based option on the barbecue has grown exponentially in the last few years. Veggie burgers are ideal as most of the accompaniments for meaty options work beautifully. This version consists of a big portobello mushroom cooked over applewood and served with melted blue cheese and smoked tomato ketchup.

1 Set a fire in a hot smoker, preheat it to the target temperature, and prime it with applewood chips.
2 Combine the oil and garlic in a bowl, then brush generously over the mushrooms. Transfer the mushrooms to the hot smoker and smoke for about 10 minutes
3 Divide the blue cheese among the mushrooms and place on the grill or into a skillet with the butter. Cook for 4–5 minutes, until the cheese is melted and the mushrooms are golden brown.
4 Sandwich in brioche rolls and serve with smoked tomato ketchup and a colourful mixed salad

SMOKED TOMATO KETCHUP

makes: 500ml/17fl oz/2 cups
difficulty: 🔥🔥
wood: mesquite
equipment: hot smoker, foil tray, foil, food processor, large pan
smoking time: 40 minutes
target temperature: 200°C/400°F
then 120°C/250°F

1kg/2¹⁄₄lb ripe tomatoes
250g/9oz shallots, halved lengthways
30ml/2 tbsp olive oil
5ml/1 tsp salt
pinch of ground black pepper
5ml/1 tsp smoked paprika
115g/4oz/¹⁄₂ cup soft light brown sugar
5ml/1 tsp chipotle paste
200ml/7fl oz/scant 1 cup cider vinegar
   (optional)

Ketchup is such a ubiquitous accompaniment, especially at a barbecue, and the tangy, vinegary, savoury sauce really does work well with many foods. However, if you really want to impress and ratchet up the smokiness, have a go at making this version, especially during summer when tomatoes are plentiful and at their best, and you may have a glut.

1 Set a fire in a hot smoker, preheat it to the target temperature, and prime it with mesquite chips.
2 Core the tomatoes and score the skins, then place on a foil tray with the onions. Drizzle over the oil and season with salt, pepper and paprika. Cover with foil, then place in the smoker for 10 minutes. Remove the foil, reduce the heat to 120°C/250°F and leave the tomatoes to smoke for another 30 minutes.
3 Once the tomatoes are darker in colour, peel them and allow to cool. Blitz until smooth in a food processor, then pour into a large pan and bring to a simmer.
4 If you want to preserve the sauce add the vinegar. Cook until reduced to the consistency you prefer, then stir in the sugar and chipotle paste. You can sieve the sauce if you like it smooth.

DIRTY ONIONS

'Dirty' foods are so-called because they have been cooked directly on hot coals and end up blackened on the outside, but soft and smoky inside. It's one of the simplest and probably one of the oldest ways to smoke food and cook with no fuss and very little effort, and it's currently all the rage. Unpeeled onions work especially well, taking on lots of smoky flavour while slowly cooking and sweetening inside their papery skins, .

makes: 4
difficulty: ♦
wood: hardwood charcoal
equipment: barbecue or open fire, tongs, knife, skillet
smoking time: 1 hour
target temperature: when the charcoal ashes over

4 white onions, skin on
50g/2oz/4 tbsp butter
5ml/1 tsp sea salt
15ml/1 tbsp finely chopped parsley, to garnish

1 Prepare a barbecue or fire pit so that the charcoal gets hot then ashes over and reaches a good temperature.
2 Place the whole onions straight on the coals. Leave for about an hour to slowly cook, turning every 15 minutes or so, until they have burnt black skins. You'll know they are cooked if you can slide a knife into them and they are soft, like a ripe tomato.
3 Take the onions off the coals and leave until cool enough to handle, then cut in half and peel off the blackened skins.
4 Place in a skillet with the butter and salt and fry until they caramelise.
5 Garnish with a sprinkling of parsley.

TRY THIS

• If you enjoy this method of ember cooking then apply the same approach to butternut squash, bell peppers, tomatoes and steaks.
• I also like to wrap up foil parcels of fruit and fish and cook them directly on the coals. Whatever your ingredient, this method is a great way to use the remaining heat on a barbecue or fire while you're winding down after cooking up a feast.

DIRTY ROSEMARY POTATOES

I first cooked these after herding cattle on horseback up on the wild moors of Cornwall, and found that when they're served with steak there is no better type of barbecued potato. Herbs are excellent as a buffer for the direct heat but also impart huge amounts of aromatic flavour. As an added bonus, you can strip off the rosemary leaves and use the stems to make rosemary skewers, which are especially good if you're cooking smaller new potatoes.

serves: 4-6
difficulty: ♦
wood: hardwood charcoal
equipment: barbecue or open fire, knife or skewers, bowl
smoking time: 1 hour
target temperature: when the charcoal ashes over

12 potatoes
15-30ml/1-2 tbsp olive oil
pinch of sea salt
pinch of cracked black pepper
24 sprigs of rosemary
6 garlic bulbs, sliced in half across the
    cloves
butter, to serve

1 Prepare a barbecue or fire pit so that the charcoal gets hot, then ashes over and reaches a good temperature.
2 Score the potatoes like a jacket potato with a cross through the top, or pierce them with a skewer, or hasselback them.
3 Combine the oil, salt and pepper in a bowl, add the potatoes and turn to coat.
4 Arrange the rosemary and garlic on the embers and then place the potatoes on top. Cook for 1 hour, turning the potatoes every 15 minutes, until they have crispy skins and are soft and fluffy inside. The herbs will burn and the potato skin will also char but they should be worth the wait.
5 Serve warm with butter and rosemary flowers to garnish, if you have some.

TRY THIS

• Sweet potato with sage is another great flavour combination, or try cooking a whole celeriac with big bunches of thyme. Try cover the top of the vegetables with extra herbs for a more intense herby aroma.
• Alternatively, if you don't have enough herbs, you can hay bake the potatoes by simply soaking the hay in a little water, spreading it on the hot embers with a generous sprinkle of sea salt, adding the potatoes and then covering them with more hay. Allow to cook for a good hour. This technique can be used for all sorts of meat, fish and other vegetables.

SMOKED CHICKPEAS

makes: 400g/14oz
difficulty: 🔥
wood: mesquite
equipment: cold smoker, bowl, foil or fine gauze
smoking time: 2–3 hours
target temperature: xx°C/xx°F

400g/14oz can of chickpeas, drained
15ml/1 tbsp olive oil

Chickpeas are an ingredient that lots of us instantly associate with hummus – a food that my family, and many others, absolutely love. However, sometimes it can be a bit bland and unadventurous as a dip, which is where smoking the chickpeas comes in. They also work in a tagine or veggie curry, but they really elevate the taste profile of hummus.

1 Prepare a cold smoker (see page 32–33), priming it with 30ml/2 tbsp mesquite chips.
2 Mix the chickpeas in a bowl with the oil, then arrange on a sheet of foil or fine gauze in the smoker.
3 Smoke for 2–3 hours, turning the chickpeas several times during the process so they are evenly smoked.
4 Store in the fridge in an airtight container if you don't use them right away.

SMOKED HUMMUS

makes: 1 large bowl
difficulty: 🔥
equipment: food processor or blender

400g/14oz smoked chickpeas
60ml/4 tbsp olive oil, plus extra to serve
2 garlic cloves, crushed or finely sliced
30ml/2 tbsp lemon juice
30ml/2 tbsp tahini
5ml/1 tsp salt
5ml/1 tsp harissa paste (optional)
paprika and warm flatbread, to serve

1 Put most of the chickpeas and all of the remaining ingredients except for the harissa paste, if using, into a food processor or blender.
2 Blitz until the mixture is as smooth as you like it.
3 Stir in the harissa paste, if you like, and drizzle over some olive oil.
4 Sprinkle with paprika, top with the reserved smoked chickpeas and serve with good bread.

TRY THIS

• The smoked chickpeas make great crunchy snacks if you roast them in a little oil and sprinkle them with salt and paprika.
• Try using butter (lima) beans instead of chickpeas, or smoke some beetroot sprinkled with cumin and blitz it with a few chopped ready-to-eat dried apricots for a colourful hummus.

SMOKED CABBAGE

makes: 1
difficulty: 🔥🔥
wood: applewood
equipment: cold smoker, boning or flexible knife,
smoking time: 3 hours
target temperature: 120°C/250°F

---

1 large red cabbage
2 sprigs of rosemary, leaves picked and finely chopped
50g/2oz/¼ cup salted butter
salt and ground black pepper

There is more to cabbage that just coleslaw! Smoked cabbage can be a delicious dish to serve alongside a glazed ham or smoked pork shoulder, or with crispy lardons of bacon and slivers of apple as a side dish that is both sweet and smoky. I also sometimes like to take it one step further and ferment the smoked cabbage to add a bright lift to the flavour and complement the darker smoke tones. This is the perfect recipe if you want to try out fermenting, and uses your brining skills, too. If you want to soften the intensity of the kraut, you can braise the fermented sauerkraut in a light stock, which reduces the acidity levels.

1 Prepare a cold smoker (see page 32–33) and prime it with applewood chips.
2 Carefully remove the core from your cabbage using a boning or other flexible knife. You are aiming to keep the cabbage intact, with a cavity down the middle.
3 Mash together the rosemary, butter and seasoning, then use most of it to stuff the cavity of the cabbage. Rub the rest on the outside of the cabbage.
4 Place in the smoker and leave for 2 hours, then cover with foil and smoke for 1 hour more.
5 Allow the cabbage to cool, then slice it thinly.

SMOKED CABBAGE KRAUT

makes: 2-4 jars
difficulty: 🔥🔥
equipment: pan, spoon, bowl, sieve, dish towel or clear film (plastic wrap), Kilner jars
fermenting time: 2 weeks
target temperature: 5°C/41°F then <23°C/73°F

---

1 litre/1¾ pints/4 cups water
65g/2½oz/5 tbsp salt
1 smoked cabbage, shredded

1 To make a brine, heat the water and salt in a pan, stirring until the salt dissolves. Allow the brine to cool, then chill in the fridge to 5°C/41°F.
2 Put the shredded smoked cabbage into a bowl and pour in the chilled brine so that it covers the cabbage. Place a sieve on top to keep cabbage submerged.
3 Cover the bowl with a dish towel or clear film and leave in a cool place for 2 weeks. The temperature should get no higher than 23°C/73°F; this will allow fermentation to begin but not enable harmful bacteria to multiply.
4 After 2 weeks, drain the brine. Your smoked kraut is now ready to eat.
5 Store in a sealed jar in the fridge for up to 3 weeks.

TRY THIS
Have a go with white cabbage instead of red. Or, for smoked fennel kraut, follow the same method as above but use fennel bulbs.

SMOKED CAULIFLOWER

makes: 1
difficulty: 🔥🔥🔥
wood: maple
equipment: hot smoker, small pan, brush, skewer
smoking time: 1–1½ hours
target temperature: 180°C/350°F

30ml/2 tbsp coconut oil
5ml/1 tsp cumin seeds
5ml/1 tsp ground turmeric
5ml/1 tsp yellow mustard seeds
pinch of salt
1 large cauliflower, trimmed of all but the most tender leaves

Cauliflower, in my opinion, is the perfect vegetable for smoking on a barbecue because it has texture, flavour and a meaty quality that keeps both vegetarians and meat-eaters happy. What's more, with a little effort you can transform it into something colourful, exciting and seriously tasty, whether served whole as a roast or split down into steaks for individual servings, the latter taking less time to smoke.

1 Set a fire in a hot smoker, preheat it to the target temperature, and prime it with maple chips.
2 Prepare a marinade by melting the coconut oil in a pan, then add the cumin seeds, turmeric, yellow mustard seeds and salt. I like to use coconut oil for this dish but other vegetable oils work well too.
3 Brush the cauliflower all over in the spiced oil and arrange on a grill in your smoker or suspended from a hook.
4 Smoke for 1–1½ hours, basting the cauliflower halfway through the cooking time in more spiced oil and turning it round.
5 The cauliflower is done when it takes on a tandoori-style blackened finish, and when it is soft in the middle when you stick a skewer in.

SMOKED CAULIFLOWER POPPERS

serves: 4
difficulty: 🔥🔥
equipment: 2 large bowls, whisk or fork, frying pan, slotted spoon, kitchen paper
cooking time: 1–1½ hours
target temperature: 180°C/350°F

1 large smoked cauliflower
50g/2oz/½ cup plain (all-purpose) flour, plus 15ml/1 tbsp for dusting
15ml/1 tbsp grated fresh root ginger
15ml/1 tbsp finely diced fresh green chilli
2.5ml/½ tsp garam masala
2.5ml/½ tsp ground turmeric
2.5ml/½ tsp baking powder
pinch of salt
50ml/2fl oz/¼ cup water or coconut milk
oil, for shallow frying
mango chutney or salsa, to serve

1 Break the smoked cauliflower florets into a large bowl and allow to cool. Dust with the 15ml/1 tbsp flour, to help the batter stick.
2 Make a spiced batter by putting the flour, ginger, chilli, spices, baking powder and salt in a large bowl and gradually adding water or coconut milk, mixing with a whisk or fork until you have a smooth batter.
3. Heat enough oil for shallow frying in a frying pan.
4 Dip the cauliflower florets into the batter and then drop them straight into the hot oil and fry for 5–10 minutes, turning regularly, until golden brown.
5 Transfer to kitchen paper to absorb any excess oil then serve hot with a mango chutney or salsa.

TRY THIS
I heartily recommend thickly slicing your smoked cauliflower and using it in a vegetarian 'steak' sandwich with some horseradish sauce, or for an Indian-inspired cauliflower cheese bake with turmeric and mustard in a Cheddar cheese sauce.

SMOKED AVOCADO

Avocado on toast is a delicious and healthy brunch but if you want to add some depth of flavour to it, then you've got to try this simple smoked avo recipe. My advice is that less is more when it comes to the smoking time, if you want to maintain a fresh green colour and keep those clean breakfast flavours. Serve as a chunky smashed version on toast or blitz until it's smoother to use as a smoky guacamole to add to your favourite burger dish, tacos or nachos.

makes: 2
difficulty: 🔥🔥
wood: maple, cherry or pecan
equipment: stove-top smoker or Dutch oven, knife, small, shallow heatproof bowl, heatproof ramekin
smoking time: 15 minutes
target temperature: medium

2 avocados

1 Prepare a stove-top smoker or Dutch oven (see page 31) and prime it with a handful of wood chips in the base. I like to use mild smoked flavours for this as I tend to eat smoked avocado as a breakfast dish, so go for more subtle tones of maple, cherry or pecan.
2 Slice the avocados and remove the stone (pit). Dice the flesh and place it in a small, shallow heatproof bowl.
3 Place an upturned ramekin in the base of the smoker or Dutch oven and position the bowl of avocado on top. Cover with a lid.
4 Place on the stove over medium heat and when you see smoke starting to be generated, set a timer for 5 minutes. When the time is up, switch off the stove and leave the avocado in the smoker for a further 10 minutes.

SMOKED AVO ON TOAST

serves: 4
difficulty: 🔥🔥
equipment: fork or potato masher, bowl

2 smoked avocados
30ml/2 tbsp chopped fresh coriander (cilantro)
10ml/2 tsp chopped fresh red chilli
2 limes
15ml/1 tbsp olive oil
pinch of salt
4 slices of sourdough bread, toasted
4 poached eggs, to serve (optional)
pinch of chipotle powder, to garnish

1 Using a fork or potato masher, roughly mix the smoked avocado with the fresh coriander, chilli and the juice from 1 lime in a bowl. Drizzle with a little oil and a pinch of salt.
2 Spoon on to the toast and top with a poached egg, if you like.
3 Garnish with a pinch of chipotle powder and serve with the remaining lime, cut into wedges.

SMOKED CHILLIES

It is possible to buy commercially smoke-dried jalapeños, sold as chipotle chillies, but it's easy to make your own. They have a wonderful intense flavour that perfectly balances smoked sweetness with warming chilli heat, and can be used in all sorts of dishes. You can try smoking any type of chilli, but in my opinion jalapeño is the best. I like to use both red and green ones, the only proviso being that they must all be ripe and in good condition.

makes: 1kg/2¼lb
difficulty: 🔥
wood: fruit or hickory
equipment: cold smoker, kitchen paper, knife, disposable gloves, tongs, conventional oven or dehydrator
smoking time: >12 hours
drying time: 12 hours
target temperature: smoker – 150°C/300°F, oven or dehydrator – 100°C/212°F

1kg/2¼lb jalapeños

TRY THIS

- If you can, leave your smoked chillies to dry out in the oven or dehydrator for 48 hours. You can then blitz them in a spice grinder and store as a chipotle chilli powder for use in soups, barbecue rubs, or even for making your own chipotle salt to season food with a distinct sweet pepper finish.
- Alternatively, you can rehydrate the smoked chillies in warm water and slice them into marinades, or use them to make a sauce.

1 Prepare a cold smoker (see page 32–33), priming it with fruit wood or hickory chips. You're aiming for a low and slow session – at least 12 hours, so prepare accordingly.

2 Wash and dry the jalapeños, then slice off the tops – this allows greater air flow to speed up the drying process and increase the smoked flavour. Because you'll be handling the peppers so much I'd recommend wearing disposable gloves. I like my chipotle with some heat so I keep the seeds in, but if you want a milder smoked chilli then remove the membrane and seeds. If you want to keep them intact, make a slit in the side with a sharp knife to allow smoke into the heart of the chilli.

3 Smoke for at least 12 hours. You may want to turn them at some point but it is best to avoid moving them too much; simply let the smoker do its work.

4 The jalapeños should be leathery to the touch, dark in colour and full of aroma when you have finished smoking them.

5 If you want to preserve them for your spice cupboard then you need to dry them out thoroughly in an oven or dehydrator overnight, until they are brittle. Alternatively, keep the smoked chillies in a sealed container in the fridge and use within 2 weeks.

SMOKED GARLIC

Smoked garlic is a great go-to ingredient and can be used in place of fresh garlic in many of your favourite recipes, including a rich garlic butter. The benefit of smoking a batch over coals is that some will end up hot smoked while the bulbs exposed to less heat will take on a more subtle flavour, and will keep for longer. This is the perfect smoking recipe for when you've finished cooking on a fire pit or barbecue, and just requires the addition of some fruity wood for smoke. You can even leave them overnight.

makes: 12
difficulty: 🔥🔥
wood: cherry
equipment: hot smoker or barbecue
smoking time: 2–3 hours
target temperature: 180°C/350°F

12 garlic bulbs

1   Prepare a hot smoker, fire pit or barbecue, and prime it with a couple of handfuls of cherry wood chips, or add the chips to live coals after you've finished smoking or cooking something else.
2   For cold-smoked garlic, position the bulbs to one side, away from direct heat, so that the smoke passes through them. For soft, intensely flavoured hot-smoked garlic, place the bulbs nearer the heat.
3   Cold smoke for 6–12 hours, and hot smoke for 2–3 hours.

serves: 6
difficulty: 🔥
equipment: mixing bowl, whisk or wooden spoon, baking parchment or clear film (plastic wrap), kitchen string

6 cloves of hot-smoked garlic, peeled
250g/9oz/generous 1 cup unsalted butter, softened
5ml/1 tsp sea salt

SMOKED GARLIC BUTTER

1   Place the smoked garlic in a mixing bowl with the butter.
2   Beat with a whisk or wooden spoon until creamed and smooth.
3   Season with salt, then spread out in a rough log shape on a sheet of baking parchment or clear film.
4   Roll into a neat cylinder about 5cm/2in in diameter, tie each end, and place in the fridge or freezer. It will keep in the fridge for up to 2 weeks, or frozen for 2–3 months.
5   Slice off discs of butter as and when you want to use it.

TRY THIS
You can combine other ingredients with your smoked garlic, such as seaweed flakes, fresh herbs or spices. Smoked garlic butter spiked with fresh chilli is especially good melted on a dirty steak or a baked potato.

SMOKED EGGS

I first tried making my own smoked eggs more than 20 years ago and have never looked back. They are one of the easiest foods to smoke at home and have a distinctive flavour and meaty texture that is quite different from that of hard-boiled eggs. For this recipe I have taken the simple approach of cold smoking the hard-boiled eggs for a couple of hours and then scooping out the yolks for a smokin' twist on deviled eggs, with paprika and mustard.

Makes: 6–12
difficulty: 🔥🔥
wood: hickory or cherry
equipment: cold smoker, pan, bowl
smoking time: 2 hours
target temperature: 110°C/225°F

6–12 eggs

1 Prepare a cold smoker (see page 32–33) and prime it with hickory or cherry wood chips. You can also add the eggs to an existing smoke, such as the chillies.
2 Meanwhile, put the eggs in a pan of cold water, bring to a simmer and cook for 7–8 minutes.
3 Drain and transfer to a bowl of cold water. Leave until just warm, then crack and peel
4 Place the eggs in the cold smoker and leave for 2 hours, until bronze in colour.

SMOKIN' DEVILED EGGS

Makes: 6
difficulty: 🔥🔥
equipment: knife, bowl, plastic piping bag or zip-lock bag

6 smoked eggs
45ml/3 tbsp mayonnaise
10ml/2 tsp finely chopped chives
5ml/1 tsp Dijon mustard
5ml/1 tsp cider vinegar
dash of sriracha hot sauce, plus extra to serve (optional)
salt and ground black pepper, to taste
pinch of paprika, to garnish

1 Carefully slice the smoked eggs in half and remove the yolks. Place in a plastic piping bag or zip-lock bag.
2 Combine the mayonnaise, chives, mustard, vinegar, sriracha and seasoning in a bowl, then add to the bag and squeeze everything together until smooth.
3 Cut a corner off the bag and pipe the mixture into the hollowed-out egg whites.
4 Garnish with paprika and serve with hot sauce on the side, if you like.

SMOKED BLUE CHEESE

Hard blue cheeses are easier to smoke than crumbly or soft ones. Being based in the Southwest, Dorset Blue Vinny or Cornish Blue are probably my two favourite types to use for this recipe. Stilton is a winner, too, and provides both a strong flavour and robust texture. Smoked blue cheese is incredibly versatile; you can use it simply on a cheese board or with a glass of port, but I also love the combination of smoked blue with duck, pear and pickled walnuts, or melted on top of a burger. Another idea is to make a smoked blue cheese and pecan pâté.

Makes: 500g/1¼lb
difficulty: 🔥🔥
wood: maple
equipment: cold smoker, knife, brush, tray of ice, baking parchment
freezing time: 10–15 minutes
smoking time: 2 hours
cooling time: 15 minutes
maturing time: 1–2 weeks
target temperature: 32°C/90°F

450g/1lb Stilton or other hard blue cheese
15ml/1 tbsp maple syrup
crackers, chutney and some sliced apple or celery, to serve

1 Prepare a cold smoker (see page 32–33) and prime it with maple chips.
2 Remove any rind from your cheese and place it in the freezer for 10–15 minutes, to bring down the temperature and help dry out the surface slightly.
3 Lightly brush the cheese with maple syrup and transfer to a cold smoker with a tray of ice below it to keep the temperature as low as possible. Smoke for 2 hours, turning the cheese every 30 minutes.
4 As soon as the smoking is finished, open the door and allow the cheese to cool in the smoker for 15 minutes.
5 Once cold, wrap the cheese in baking parchment and leave it in the fridge for 1–2 weeks. Don't be tempted to try it before this time as it may taste bitter until the smoked flavour has been absorbed and has had a chance to mellow.
6 Serve with crackers, chutney and some sliced apple or celery.

SMOKED FIGS

makes: 12
difficulty: 🔥🔥
wood: applewood
equipment: cold smoker, knife, brush
smoking time: 20-30 minutes
target temperature: 95°C/203°F

12 figs
15ml/1 tbsp walnut oil

Figs are a robust fruit to smoke and their sweetness takes on woody flavours really well. Adding some fresh thyme or rosemary to the smoking wood chips adds a perfumed quality to the finished product. They are perfect served on a cheese board, turned into a smoky fig jam or combined with creamy Brie and served in a crisp filo pastry cup.

1 Prepare a cold smoker (see page 32-33) and prime it with applewood chips.
2 Slice the figs in half lengthways and brush with a little oil - walnut oil is my favourite for this method.
3 Smoke for 20-30 minutes, until softened and tender.

SMOKED FIG AND BRIE PARCELS

makes: 8
difficulty: 🔥🔥
equipment: conventional oven, knife, muffin tin (pan), pastry brush
cooking time: 20 minutes

8 filo pastry sheets
50g/2oz/¼ cup salted butter, melted
4 smoked figs, halved
200g/7oz Brie, sliced
10ml/2 tsp chopped fresh thyme
10ml/2 tsp clear honey

1 Preheat the oven to 180°C/350°F/Gas 4.
2 Cut the filo pastry sheets into squares measuring about 10 x 10cm/4 x 4in.
3. Layer the first pastry squares in eight holes of a muffin tin, brush with a little butter, then repeat with the next pastry square. Continue, altering the angle of the square each time, until you've layered three of four squares of pastry and created eight filo cups.
4 Place half a smoked fig in the middle and a slice of Brie on either side.
5 Sprinkle with a pinch of chopped thyme and a drizzle of honey.
6 Bake for about 20 minutes, until the pastry is crisp and golden and the Brie has melted. Keep a close eye on them as filo can burn very easily

SMOKED STRAWBERRIES

serves: 4–6
difficulty: 🔥🔥
wood: 2 well-seasoned oak logs
equipment: barbecue, rack and roasting tray (optional)
smoking time: 20–30 minutes
target temperature: residual heat after cooking everything else

900g/2lb strawberries

Smoked strawberries are the perfect way to end a meal and make great use of residual heat after you've finished working the main course. I usually like to throw a couple of well-seasoned hardwood logs on the coals of the barbecue, and these serve both as a smoke producer and a trivet on which I can place a baking tray loaded with strawberries. Alternatively, you can just put the strawberries straight on the log, if it has a flat side that they won't roll off, or use a smoking plank. You then close the lid of the barbecue and allow the berries to smoke for 20–30 minutes, just until they have taken on the smoke but retain a bit of bite. They are scrumptious on their own, and even better served with pepper-spiked meringues

1 Place the oak logs on the embers of a barbecue or fire pit.
2 Arrange the strawberries evenly on a rack in a roasting tray or straight on the logs. If you do the latter, ensure they aren't in contact with direct heat and allow room for the smoke to circulate around the fruit.
3 Smoke for 20–30 minutes.

BLACK PEPPER MERINGUE AND SMOKED STRAWBERRY MESS

serves: 4–6
difficulty: 🔥🔥
equipment: conventional oven, 2 large baking sheets, baking parchment, electric whisk, grease-free large bowl
cooking time: 2¼ hours

6 egg whites
350g/12oz/1¾ cups caster (superfine) sugar
2.5ml/½ tsp cracked black pepper
300ml/½ pint/1¼ cups clotted cream
smoked strawberries
drizzle of orange liqueur (optional)

1 Preheat the oven to 150°C/300°F/Gas 2. Line the baking sheets with baking parchment.
2 Whisk the egg whites in a grease-free large bowl to form soft peaks.
3 Add one-third of the sugar and continue to whisk for several minutes.
4 Gradually incorporate another one-third of the sugar, a spoonful at a time, until the mixture forms stiff peaks.
5 Fold in the remaining sugar and the black pepper. The mixture should now be smooth and glossy.
6 Shape the mixture into about 16 large meringue blobs on the lined baking sheets.
7 Bake for 15 minutes, then reduce the temperature to 110°C/225°F/Gas ¼ and leave in the oven for another 2 hours, until crisp and dry.
8 Leave to cool, then serve with smoked strawberries and clotted cream, drizzled with orange liqueur, if using.

TRY THIS
You can preserve these smoked strawberries in a jar for a smoky, fruit-infused version of Rumtopf by weighing the fruit, then measuring out half that weight in caster (superfine) sugar and combining the two. Place in a sterilised jar and cover with orange liqueur or rum.

SMOKED NUTS

Smoked almonds are probably my favourite smoked nuts, ticking all the boxes with their salty, sweet and smoky tones, but cashews and peanuts also work really well. By smoking the nuts after roasting them, you add fabulous depth of flavour for sweet or savoury dishes. Almonds are delicious chopped and served simply with bread, oil and a sprinkle of za'atar as a rustic starter, cashews make a delicious nut butter, and peanuts add crunch and flavour to a spicy satay sauce.

makes: 500g/1¼lb
difficulty: 🔥🔥
wood: hickory dust
equipment: cold smoker, oven, baking tray, small pan, baking tray, foil
roasting time: 10–12 minutes
smoking time: 4 hours
target temperature: oven – 180°C/350°F/Gas 4, cold smoker – 15–30°C/59–86°F

500g/1¼lb skin-on almonds
75g/3oz/6 tbsp salted butter
60ml/4 tbsp granulated sugar
10ml/2 tsp sea salt flakes

BUTTERED ALMONDS

1 Prepare a cold smoker (see page 32–33), priming it with hickory dust. Preheat a standard oven.
2 Roast the almonds on a baking tray in the preheated oven for 10–12 minutes, keeping a close eye on them to prevent them from burning.
3 Melt the butter in a small pan and pour over the almonds. Add the sugar and salt and stir thoroughly to coat .
4 Line the baking tray with foil and tip the almonds on to it, spreading them out evenly.
5 Position at the top of the smoker and cold smoke for 4 hours.
6 After smoking, leave the nuts to cool, then store them in an airtight container. Or eat them straight out of the smoker!

TRY THIS

For something completely different, blitz the smoked nuts until smooth and serve with strawberry and black pepper jam on Belgian waffles and bacon.

equipment: cold smoker, bowl, foil-lined tray, kitchen paper
smoking time: 2 hours
target temperature: 95°C/203°F

500g/1¼lb peanuts
15ml/1 tbsp groundnut oil
5ml/1 tsp sea salt

SMOKED PEANUTS

Smoked peanuts make a welcome change from plain roasted ones as a snack on their own, but they can also be added to salads or made into a delicious smoky satay sauce that works really well in a stir-fry, brushed on to char-grilled chicken, or with marinated tofu in a hot noodle salad (see next page).

1 Preheat a cold smoker (see page 32–33) and prime it with cherry shavings.
2 Coat the peanuts in the oil in a bowl, then spread out on a foil-lined tray.
3 Smoke for 2 hours, until the peanuts are darker in colour, then place on a sheet of kitchen paper to drain and cool. Eat or store in an airtight container.

TRY THIS

• Have a go at smoking seeds. You need to smoke pumpkin and sunflower seeds for just 2 hours.
• For best results, make sure the nuts are always coated with oil or butter, as here, before smoking them.

SMOKED SATAY SAUCE

1 Heat the oil in a wok or frying pan, then add the onion. Cook for about 10 minutes, until golden, then add the chilli and garlic and cook for 2-3 minutes.
2 Add the smoked peanuts, lime juice, soy sauce and sugar and stir to combine.
3 Blitz in a food processor or blender for 2 minutes on pulse, until the sauce is as smooth as you like it. I prefer a coarse texture. Transfer to a jar.
4 Serve with any kind of crisp vegetable stir fry and scatter with a few more whole smoked peanuts for added crunch.

serves: 4
difficulty: 🔥🔥
equipment: wok or frying pan, food processor or blender
cooking time: 12-13 minutes

15ml/1 tbsp coconut oil
1/2 white onion, finely chopped
1 fresh red chilli, seeded and finely chopped
1 garlic clove, finely chopped
115g/4oz smoked peanuts
juice of 1 lime
30ml/2 tbsp soy sauce
10ml/2 tsp soft light brown sugar

SMOKED CASHEW NUT BUTTER

makes: 500g/1¼lb
difficulty: 🔥🔥
equipment: food processor, pan
processing time: about 5 minutes

500g/1¼lb smoked cashews (see
    smoked almonds, page 162)
30ml/2 tbsp coconut oil
10ml/2 tsp caster (superfine) sugar
pinch of salt

Peanut butter has stolen the limelight for years, but there is now a nutty revolution happening with all sorts of other nut butters gaining in popularity. I like to incorporate coconut oil for its flavour but peanut or vegetable oil are fine to use, too.

1 Put the smoked cashews in a food processor and blitz until a smooth butter comes together. This should take 3–4 minutes, unless you like a rougher-textured nut butter.
2 Melt the coconut oil in a pan, then pour it in a steady stream into the running food processor.
3 Add the sugar and salt and blitz one last time.
4 Serve immediately – it's especially good on toast with smashed avocado – or transfer it to a sterilised jar and store in the fridge for 1–2 weeks.

ACKNOWLEDGEMENTS

To write a book you have to build a bubble around yourself and lock yourself away from time to time in order to concentrate and focus. For helping me do this at home, I'd like to thank my wife Holly for helping to provide the creative space and for letting me use all her gorgeous home-made pottery, and our children Indy, Pippin and Arrietty for being quiet – or at least quieter, sometimes – when I've been working in my office. Or perhaps I'm conveniently forgetting all the recorder tooting and bell ringing coming from downstairs...

I deliberately set out to shoot this manual to reflect the communal style that is inherent with barbecue cooking and smoking, and as a collaboration with my close friends and local suppliers. Working with Tia and Richard at Botelet (www.botelet.com), using their beautiful farm, kitchen and dairy as a location has been an absolute pleasure and I'm so incredibly grateful for all your support and for opening your home to me. Simon Burt, the superb photographer for this book, has gone beyond what I'd hoped for and become a friend who has helped shape the book's easy-going vibe by being open and capturing the really personal moments as well as finished

dishes. I'd also like to thank Simon's wife, Anna, who has come along when we needed a boost and given us an external perspective, shooting content for social media and behind the scenes.

The hands pictured in this book aren't all just mine and that's because I wanted the recipes and methods to come alive and reflect the fact that smoking food is about community and friends. Dominic Bond helped me out on a few shoots, running around, checking smokers and being my sous chef and model, as did Ed and Nema Hart, who also hosted our celebratory smoking feast on the last day of shooting. Cornish chef Aj Bartnicki also joined the kitchen brigade for a day. Thank you to all of you for getting involved and adding some fun to the whole project.

I'm so proud of my Cornish suppliers and want to express special thanks to Andrew and Sue at Tywardreath Butchers and their great team for supplying such fantastic meat and

game – and always helping me out with unusual short-notice requests. Thanks to Cornish Sea Salt for a couple of extra buckets of salt crystals when I needed them, Tregothnan for their excellent-quality British charcoal, and Richards in Par for supplying Cornish seafood and local vegetables.

I also want to say thank you to Ty and the team at ProQ Smokers, who helped with some specialist equipment, wood chips and support for the book project. They make the best smokers on the market and have been a great bunch to work with (www.proqsmokers.com).

Last but not least: Joanne, the editor, thank you for supporting me through a tough time with some unfortunate personal events and trouble in Pasty world, for your patience, and for reworking the book to make sense!

Cheers

James

Instagram: @jgstrawbridge
Twitter: @eco_boy

INDEX